ADULT DRAMA

AND OTHER ESSAYS

NATALIE BEACH

HANOVER
SQUARE
PRESS

HANOVER
SQUARE
PRESS™

ISBN-13: 978-1-335-91402-6

Adult Drama

"Self-Centered" was originally published as "I Was Caroline Calloway" in *The Cut*
on September 10, 2019.

Quoted material in the epigraph is from Molly Brodak's poem titled "Midwest Wilderness"
from poetry collection *A Little Middle of the Night*, published on March 15, 2010, by
University of Iowa Press.

Hanover Square Press
22 Adelaide St. West, 41st Floor
Toronto, Ontario M5H 4E3, Canada
HanoverSqPress.com
BookClubbish.com

Printed in U.S.A.

To my family—Mom, Dad, Charlotte and Chris.

And to Caroline Rosenstone, a fabulous teacher.

I met a former friend at some distance:
she put on her hat like *if you're different*

then I am too. I forgot her lake-wave hair,
and frowned out *I'm not lonely either.*

—Molly Brodak, "Midwest Wilderness"

"Every day takes figuring out all over again how to fucking live."

—Calamity Jane, *Deadwood*

CONTENTS

AUTHOR'S NOTE

This collection was written between 2020 and 2022.
What a time.

In certain instances, names were changed and dialogue
approximated. The essays are meant to stand alone,
although they certainly jostle against each other,
and here and there cover the same time period from
different angles.

DISTRESSED DENIM

There are no atheists in an Abercrombie dressing room. And so I prayed, shivery and pubescent, half naked in a mirrored box the size of a confessional. *Please fit, please look good for one goddamn time.*

"How's it going in there, babe?" my soccer teammates sang from their huddle on the other side of the door. Meanwhile, I toppled over as I stuffed my foot into a pair of bootcut jeans.

I told them I was "on the fence." So judicious! As if I was merely buying pants instead of locked in confrontation with all that was wrong with my body. I knew my parents would rather go quail hunting with Dick Cheney (this was 2006) than fork over ninety dollars for one pair of pants. I also knew these jeans would never fit me. I was fourteen years old and had knobby knees and a ludicrous bubble butt that a three-inch rise could not cover, no matter how hard I willed it. Inevitably, though, any weekend my team wasn't playing in Massapequa or deep in Jersey, I found myself peer-pressured into an underlit and overcologned store, where I'd once again try to cram myself into a pair of hip-huggers, pleading that the denim would stretch just enough to allow me to zip myself into the shape of a girl.

As a kid, all I cared about was soccer. I was an absolute freak for it. My middle school teachers insisted I stop writing book reports exclusively on Michelle Akers biographies. My most prized possession was a slice of Mia Hamm's birthday cake I kept preserved in the freezer. (A gift from a sporty aunt who worked tangentially with the WUSA.) Every day after school I played two-v-two streetball, neighborhood brothers and my sister and I, using driveways as goals and porch lights to keep going until dinner (or until a boy went home crying). On the weekends I played for my travel team and the New Haven boys league; during holiday breaks there was pickup with the local dads in East Rock Park; and in the winter I moved to small-sided games in a climate-controlled plastic bubble that rose like a giant white head above Route 80. In those days, I could recite the starting lineup of the 1999 Women's National Team, and had never heard of Abercrombie & Fitch. I didn't even own a pair of jeans! I wore soccer shorts most of the school year, in shiny primary colors with an elastic waist and drawstring. They swooshed in time with my ponytail, they had stripes, they wicked away sweat. They were perfect clothes.

I was forced to wear a skirt exactly once a year, on the first day of school, because as my mom insisted, "You only have one chance to make a first impression." She didn't understand that I chose my outfits not for how they made me look but what they allowed me to do— bike to school, absolutely wreck kids in gym class, etc. The other girls wore Limited Too polo shirts and pink denim jackets. They straightened their hair and touched up their lip gloss with those plastic applicators, sticky as fly paper. And then the jeans. Everyone was wearing them and they seemed needlessly uncomfortable, held together with cold metal zippers and snaps or suede cor- setry, embellished with rhinestone butterflies, flaring out over ballet flats or Heelys (well, until those were banned by the principal).

The other eighth grade girls were the same age as I was, but a different species. One after another, they switched from overalls and jumpers to low-rise jeans, got their pe- riods, first kisses, underwire bras, became teenagers. And good for them! These were my friends and classmates, and we were all Worthington Hooker Middle School kids buying our clothes secondhand or on markdown, eating the same free New Haven public school lunches. Half the kids were immigrants from Bangladesh, Japan, Botswana, Poland, and our parents slapped bumper stick- ers on their cars that read Proud Hooker Mom. I dressed in graphic T-shirts from the soccer catalog Eurosport and my classmates still voted me Eighth Grade President. I only wish I'd known how good I had it.

I was still in diapers when designer Lee Alexander McQueen kicked off the modern lust for low-rise jeans. At the bombastic start of his career, McQueen sent models down the London catwalk in dresses made from chicken wire, whited-out contact lenses, and bumsters—slacks cut so low they revealed the wearer's "bum cleavage." The high fashion plumber's cracks, and the shows they debuted in, were quite the scandal, with critics unsure what to make of collections that looked like evidence in a murder trial. Reviewing McQueen's 1995 show "Highland Rape" for *The Independent*, Marion Hume wrote, "models who look as if they have recently experienced serious traffic accidents, in sheer and sweaty cling film knickers, with what appeared to be bloody, suppurating, post-operative breasts visible through muslin T-shirts, was rather a lot to take in the name of frocks." Which was the reaction desired by the "hooligan of English fashion," who before the show instructed models to put their "pubic hair in Anna Wintour's face."

As critics argued that the torn dresses and yanked-down trousers in "Highland Rape" romanticized misogyny, McQueen insisted they were missing the point. Though his work sprang from a capacious reference base—Hitchcock, Joan of Arc, *Charlie's Angels*, Bruegel the Elder, Travis Bickle, punk, porn, grindhouse, Dolly Parton, Tom of Finland—in the end McQueen's designs always found their way back to his own life. "My father's family originates from the Isle of Skye, and I'd studied the history of the Scottish upheavals and the Clearances," he told *Time Out* magazine. "People were so unintelligent they thought this was about women being raped—yet 'Highland Rape' was about England's rape of Scotland." And also: "I've seen a woman get nearly beaten to death by her husband... I hate this thing about fragility and making women feel naive... I want people to be afraid of the women I dress." And also: "We're not talking about models' feelings here. We're talking about mine."

McQueen grew up a chubby kid with teeth, a friend remembered, like Stonehenge. He described himself as the "pink sheep" of the family and was called "McQueer" and much worse by his classmates. He routinely saw his sister get beaten by her husband, the same man who sexually abused McQueen. Years later, McQueen would describe the trauma obliquely: "I gave adults a lot of time in my life when I was young and some of them hurt me." His biographer Andrew Wilson writes, McQueen "began to fuse his experiences with [his sister's]. Both of them had suffered abuse at the hands of the same man and he felt the need to purge the stew of feelings—anger, revenge, despair, corruption, guilt and fragmentation—that he felt growing inside him." Fashion design would not only give him the means to escape his circumstances, but allow McQueen to recast the ugliness of his childhood into sartorial armor.

After fashion school and an apprenticeship at the hoity-toity tailor Gieves & Hawkes—he'd later claim to have chalked "McQueen was here" and "I am a cunt" in the lining of Prince Philip's jacket—McQueen began producing his own collections. At chaotic, grungy shows he presented work meant to appall the fashion establishment. "If I get someone like Suzy Menkes in the front row, wearing her fucking Christian Lacroix, I make sure the lady gets pissed on by one of the girls," he said. "I always try to slam ideas in people's faces." He stitched human hair into garments inspired by Jack the Ripper, filled acrylic bodices with wet, writhing worms. He'd dress models in impeccably constructed couture and then roll a tire covered in paint across the women just before they stepped on stage. Nowhere was his ability to marry classical design with the obscene more realized than his famous bumsters. The trousers referenced the sixteenth century patterns of Basque mathematician and tailor Juan de Alcega and William Hogarth's "Line of Beauty" theory, as well as the styles of pants worn by construction workers and gay hustlers. That said, McQueen insisted the design wasn't meant to show off the wearer's ass, but rather highlight the bottom of the spine and reimagine a standard silhouette. "It was an art thing, to change the way women looked, just by cut, to make a longer torso," said McQueen. "But I was taking it to an extreme. The girls looked quite menacing, because there was so much top and so little bottom, because of the length of the legs."

In her 1994 *New York Times* review "In London, Designers Are All Grown-Ups," Amy Spindler praised McQueen's perfectly sculpted jackets, but considered the bumsters impractical and a failure. "His big trouser idea was a waistline that fell below the bikini line. It is strange to see so talented a designer so committed to the un-wearable," she wrote. "Especially when he is getting the sort of attention that usually leads to healthy careers."

Of course, Spindler was dead wrong. Unwearable or not, low-rise trousers helped launch McQueen's brand, and the style soon dominated pop culture. When Ma-donna wore bumsters for a 1994 MTV commercial, she was leading a parade of celebrities embracing the barely-there rise, the trend intersecting with the low-slung jeans already worn in the world of R & B and hip-hop, with artists like Aaliyah, Lil' Kim, Beyoncé, and J.Lo serving hip bones and belly chains on the red carpet and episodes of *Cribs*. Across the country, navel piercings, tramp stamps, and whale tails proliferated. Bikini waxes became de ri-gueur. Millennium approaches. Mariah Carey ripped the waistline off her jeans for the "Heartbreaker" video, later claiming (falsely) to have popularized the style and regret-ting she didn't take out a patent. Sisqó released "Thong Song." Liposuction became the most popular cosmetic surgery in America. In 2001 Britney Spears performed "I'm a Slave 4 U" at the VMAs with an albino Burmese python and wearing bejeweled hot pants stretched across her pelvic V, tight as cling wrap. "All you people look at me like I'm a little girl / Well did you ever think it'd be okay / For me to step into this world?" sang the nineteen-year-old. To prepare for the performance, she told MTV she did 500 sit-ups a day. "And if I'm having a really good day, I'll probably do 1,000," she said. "Muffin top" enters the lexicon. I enter high school.

When I wasn't at school, I spent every scrap of free time playing for the Connecticut Football Club (or CFC, which was confusing, because chlorofluorocarbons were really in the news). The club was expensive and elite and drew girls from across the Nutmeg State, girls that could seriously play. They were thirteen-year-olds scoring header goals and pulling off combination plays; I could start a give-and-go with Leanne at the top of our own eighteen and know that Kerry was already countering down the left flank looking to meet my through ball in stride. If that's gobbledygook to you just know it meant everything to me.

My new teammates were from the suburbs, towns like East Haven and Hamden where the New Haven cops lived, and then up the coast to lacrosse and Sperry country, Guilford and Madison, and finally, the trust-fund girls from the *Ice Storm* part of the state, where team sleepovers were hosted in palatial finished basements and my teammates were chauffeured to practice in private cars. When it came to soccer, these girls were as competitive as I was, devoting their evenings and weekends to the game, sharing in my vendettas against our rivals and the referees who crossed us. We had so much in common, almost anything that mattered, and yet whenever we weren't on the field I was a step behind, like a forward who could never anticipate the off-sides trap.

As a starting center mid-fielder, I was too integral

to the team's success to get bullied, but my existence still seemed to baffle my teammates. Like when I announced that my leg hair had grown in the shape of my shin guards. Or when I mistook Adam Brody for a Liverpool forward. Strangest of all, when we went to team dinners at TGI Fridays, I came dressed in my sports clothes—Adidas tracksuits, post-game sandals, my perfect swishy shorts. I had assumed soccer girls wore soccer outfits all the time, but I soon realized that when we weren't playing my teammates dressed in layered polo shirts, wife beaters (that's what we called them!), Uggs, and Havaianas, and to a person, skintight, predistressed, ass-hugging, low-riding jeans, all stamped with that ubiquitous moose. At first I thought of Abercrombie more like the clothing worn by foreign dignitaries to a state dinner: the traditional dress of a culture not my own that I respected while not understanding. But then there it was, sharp as menstrual cramps, those first adolescent pangs of not fitting in.

A summer night, a cul-de-sac in Darien. At a team BBQ, we scattered across the neighborhood in a game of hide-and-seek. As I watched my teammates duck behind mailboxes and hedges, I decided to show them how we played in New Haven. I thought they'd congratulate me for winning when they finally found me, wedged beneath Kelly's mom's Audi. I had been on my stomach under the car for the last thirty minutes, stifling my laughs as I watched feet pass inches from my head. When I eventually was spotted and pulled myself out, everyone was horrified. "Oh my god, why did Nat go so hard?" they wanted to

know. I thought it was obvious: Because we were playing a game and the point was to win? I wiped motor oil
off my cheek and my teammates made eye contact behind
my back and fake-dialed 911. I was a starting player on
the best U-13 soccer team in the state, but I didn't understand that while we were young enough to still play hide-
and-seek, we were too old to try. In fact, these girls were
only pretending to play one game while actually playing
another, and I was just naturally supposed to pick up on
that? It was a minor incident, but I replayed the faux pas
over and over—my giddy anticipation, their jeers when
they found me under the car. Only a maniac would think
winning a children's game was worth ruining their outfit.
I should never have made a spectacle of myself, I realized,
concluding that the problems with my teammates would
only get worse unless I figured out how to disguise myself as one of them.

"In every school there are the cool and popular kids,
and then there are the not-so-cool kids," Abercrombie
CEO Michael Jeffries infamously told a reporter for *Salon*.
"Candidly, we go after the cool kids. We go after the at-
tractive all-American kid with a great attitude and a lot of
friends." This is the kind of thing you can say to the press
when you've turned a dead sporting goods store into a five-
billion-dollar company. Under Jeffries's leadership, Abercrombie had achieved total cultural saturation. Together
the brand family—Abercrombie, Hollister, Abercrombie
& Fitch, and Ruehl No.925—totaled over eight hundred
locations. The store was featured in the chorus of LFO's hit

song "Summer Girls." Pre-fame Taylor Swift, Channing Tatum, and Ashton Kutcher were featured in Abercrombie photo spreads. In an episode of *Gossip Girl*, Abercrombie model Ashley Hinshaw cameoed as herself, prompting Blair to yell, "You may have an Abercrombie campaign… but that doesn't give you the right to steal someone else's man!" The brand magalogue, *A&F Quarterly*, drew contributions from Michael Chabon, Amy Sedaris, Bret Easton Ellis, and Margaret Cho; Slavoj Žižek wrote on *Fight Club* and the Hilton sisters considered whether they'd rather be fat or poor. Even if you didn't shop there, Abercrombie culture was inescapable and ubiquitous; after the Columbine shooting, a writer at the *Denver Post* wondered if the murders were a retaliation against the world that Jeffries created, noting that the trench-coat-wearing outcasts "committed the social sin of being very shy and different in a homogenized high school some kids called 'Abercrombie High.'"

Jeffries was accustomed to these sorts of accusations. At Abercrombie he racked up condemnations from the Catholic League, Mexican American Legal Defense, NOW, the governor of Illinois, the Asian American Association, high school "girlcotts," NAACP, and vegans, to name but a few. To Jeffries, anyone who took offense was just being cynical, and Jeffries hated cynicism, had no time for it. He was building an empire, one in which everyone was young and beautiful and carefree, and if they wore clothes at all they were dressed in flip-flops and distressed denim hanging low on their hips, exactly what Jeffries himself wore every day to work because as he told *Salon*, "Dude, I'm not an old fart who wears his jeans up at his shoulders." At the time, he was sixty-one years old.

Abercrombie Co. was founded over a century earlier. The New York store sold sporting goods and outdoor apparel, and became a shopping destination for experienced adventurers—Teddy Roosevelt, Richard Byrd, Amelia Earhart—in addition to civilians who wanted to pretend they were made of tougher stuff. The twelve-story Madison Avenue flagship boasted an armored rifle range, a log cabin on the roof (that Ezra Fitch, who joined the company in 1900, used as a townhouse), and pool large enough for Manhattanites to take fly-fishing lessons. You could walk in off the street and buy elephant guns, hot air balloons, first aid kits for dogs, apparel for hunting, sailing, skiing, and safari. Even more exotic, Abercrombie became the first store in New York to stock sports clothing for both men and women. In 1945, Lillian Ross visited the store with Ernest Hemingway as he shopped for a belt and repeatedly punched himself in the stomach. "Gee, he's got a hard tummy," remarked the sales clerk as he measured Papa's waist.

Indulge me this fantasy, an alternate reality where teens queue around the mall to buy compasses and cashmere hunting underwear. Ultimately, it was for the best that by the mid-1970s, Americans no longer wanted to dress like Rudyard Kipling. Clothing companies would have us believe that becoming a new person is as easy as swiping a credit card, but meaningful change isn't transactional. As sales tanked, Abercrombie tried halfheartedly to move with the times. They added a sale section, opened suburban locations, even considered the drastic step of stocking blue jeans, but felt that was too extreme for their customers. Instead, the company's president, former Wilmington, Delaware mayor Harry Garner Haskell Jr., planned to resuscitate the brand with a product of his own design, a hybrid of a poncho and parka called—Henry, no—a "parcha." As described in the *New York Times*, "if you like looking like a French cop, you'll love the parcha, especially when the cape is lengthened as Mr. Haskell plans." One year later the company filed for bankruptcy. Sometimes it's easier to just give up than become something different.

When retail magnate Les Wexner bought Abercrombie in 1988, what was once the largest sporting goods store in the world had been reduced to an office littered with dusty croquet sets. At the time, Jeffries didn't look like himself, either. He ran Alcott & Andrews, a floundering store marketed as Brooks Brothers for women. He had a wife and son. He went to work each day in gray flannel pants and a double-breasted navy blazer. "I don't think he ever changed his clothes," remembered a former colleague. "All that seemed to matter to him was the success of the brand." When he was hired to take over Abercrombie Jeffries ditched the blazer and dressed exclusively in the youthful clothes Abercrombie sold. He spent his mornings lifting weights barefoot in the company gym, quietly separated from his wife, and moved in with Matthew Smith, his younger life partner. He devoted himself body and soul to the company, and was known to come to work with his face still swollen from cosmetic surgery. His teeth became gleaming white, hair blond, skin unnaturally tanned and wrinkle-free, lips puffed. It was as if Jeffries was transforming himself into his ideal customer.

It must not have been fun to have been born gay in Oklahoma in 1944. I can understand Jeffries's fantasy of a do-over, this time as the blondest, richest, most popular guy around. It was this longing that made him the perfect person to sell clothes to teenagers. "Unlike his peers, who tended to view the youth market with clinical detachment, Jeffries has a Peter Pan–like ability to commune with the whims of the average American teen," wrote *New York Magazine*. "He was able to predict what his customers desired because that's what he desired too."

The stores Jeffries designed for Abercrombie looked like brothels fronting as surf shacks. Paneled in dark wood, they were disorienting and ambrosial, thrumming with club music. Black shutters over the window blocked out the mall's fluorescent light, as if shoppers were sheltering from a summer storm. Jeffries kept the stores so dark I remember holding jeans under my portable book light just to read the price tag. "It's just like the velvet rope in front of the nightclub," a retail consultant told the *Times*. "It makes people even more anxious to go inside and look." They were spaces of exclusivity, a nightclub for kids years away from turning twenty-one, where you could spend money while feeling special. To work inside the stores, Jeffries hired louche, sun-kissed teenagers. Their work performance was incidental; all that mattered was that they had the Abercrombie look. Outside the store, shirtless male models greeted customers, guys recruited from local fraternities and college sports teams (their headshots sent to upper management for approval). The hottest white boy I knew growing up—a lacrosse phenom and heir to a hotdog dynasty—was rumored to have been scouted by Abercrombie, which only made him hotter. When *New York Times* reporter Mark Albo sojourned to the SoHo Hollister, he described a pleasure palace staffed by *Baywatch* extras: "On the stairway I was greeted again by male and female models in bathing suits. The music was so loud I could only hear the guy say 'agency…modeling…weird,' his rump peeking out from the top of his board shorts."

Mock retail spaces were built at Abercrombie HQ in New Albany, Ohio, allowing Jeffries to inspect and approve every element of a display before instructions were sent off to stores across the country. No detail was too small. One button was to be undone on hanging blouses, two buttons if folded. Bras were meant to be displayed in drawers, as Jeffries thought that "big mounds of foam coming at you" was offensive. The jeans displayed on mannequins were to be as low on the hips as possible. Under no circumstances could women's clothes look butch. A former merchandiser remembered Jeffries's disapproval over a pair of corduroy pants. "Who the fuck are you designing for? Dykes on trikes?" he said.

The good-looking people who worked at the stores were also subject to Jeffries's exactitude. The staff lookbook mandated acceptable shades of makeup and nail polish, the correct size of a jean cuff (1.25 inches for men, seven-eighths of an inch for women), and how to properly scrunch shirt sleeves. Explicitly forbidden: dreadlocks, gold chains, hairstyles that don't "reflect natural beauty," conspicuous tattoos, mustaches, ankle bracelets, earrings that dangle. This was all enforced by surprise blitzes from corporate reps, and often Jeffries himself. "Life stops and starts with what Mike Jeffries says," said an employee. "There is nothing that is not shown to him, and there is nothing that he does not know about." As if by royal decree, the obsessions and insecurities of one man out in the Ohio woods echoed out across the malls of America, inescapable as that underwater sonar driving whales to suicide.

In order to sell a fantasy, people need to know what they're missing out on. For that, Jeffries brought in photographer Bruce Weber. If you've ever caught yourself falling into the glistening pectorals on an Abercrombie shopping bag, you can thank Weber, the photographer Jeffries entrusted the marketing campaigns and in-store photographs, those sumptuous soft-core portraits of America's varsity athletes in various states of undress. Raised in a mining town outside Pittsburgh, Weber was often left home alone, and he first came to photography by studying the snapshots his parents took of their world adventures without him. "I had an enormous fantasy life," he told *Vanity Fair*, "and really wanted to be as athletic or as handsome or as muscular as the people in my pictures." As a struggling artist, Weber caught his break when Diane Arbus liked a photo he took of a couple going at it in a room filled with birds. Calvin Klein launched his underwear line with Weber's famous portrait of Brazilian pole vaulter Tomás Hintnaus—tanned, bulging. He became known for his edgy black-and-white editorials of beefcakes in repose and androgynous women. A senior editor at *Ad Week* summed it up: "his photos make straight people think they're missing something."

But when Weber teamed up with Abercrombie, mainstream consumers could finally experience the charged eroticism of gay pinups, but now safely transposed onto hetero imagery: touch football, vintage cars, guys macking on chicks. Sure, Weber's photographs for Abercrombie featured naked men frolicking in fields, close-ups of parted lips, emotionally vacant and half-lidded eyes, pleasure trails, sweat-dappled torsos, and wherever you looked, denim hanging off jutting pelvic bones, as if the viewer was interrupting a strip tease, and yet!—the "no homo" generation of the mid-aughts spent billions of dollars on the same clothes that those models were hardly wearing. This was a time, remember, when homophobia was socially acceptable. The girls on my soccer team threw around slurs and called out the "manliness" of our opponents. Even the more PC of us touted our "gaydar," which is why we knew Abercrombie wasn't gay. The brand was too popular to be queer. Too enthralled with the Ivy League, America, good clean fun, whiteness. Even the colonial remnants from the brand's first iteration made it clear that Abercrombie was on the winning side.

In a 1931 issue of the *New Yorker*, E. B. White described

Abercrombie as carrying the "clothes men want to wear all the time and don't; they carry the residual evidence of what men used to be before they became what they are." While at first glance the clubby stores and homoerotic photographs of Jeffries's Abercrombie seemed to be about sex, Jeffries understood that an aspirational brand wasn't about libido, or even the price point, but the ache to be someone different, someone who belongs. The suburban storefronts designed to look like California surf shacks, flip-flops worn throughout the Ohio winter. There's a reason why so much of Abercrombie's merchandise consisted of uniforms. The Hollister Surf Team, Rocky's Longboard Camp, the Abercrombie & Fitch Athletic Department, football and rugby jerseys for teams that didn't exist but still won every game. Buy the right prewashed denim and you can transform yourself into a California surfer, a WASP, a heterosexual, all-American. Wear the right uniform and you're on the team. (In his last journal entry, one of the Columbine shooters wrote, "I hate you people for leaving me out of so many fun things.") As a boy, Jeffries broke his father's heart for being bad at basketball, but the year he said to *Salon* "Are we exclusionary? Absolutely," Abercrombie made almost two billion dollars.

I will never be as thin as I was in high school, but that kind of perspective couldn't survive the rat trap of a dressing room. On weekends my dad gave me a twenty-dollar bill and I carpooled out to the Westfield Mall, where my teammates crowded into Abercrombie and Hollister and loaded my arms with jeans I could neither afford nor for some reason, fit into. I was an athletic white girl, and so, unlike a lot of people, Abercrombie actually carried my size. And yet, no matter how I shimmied or sucked in or sized up, why did these jeans still not work for me? Was it my bad attitude? Perhaps the same invisible deficiency that my teammates sensed, the inadequacy that kept me separate from them and stuck in a perpetual state of misunderstanding. Maybe I had the yips, but for how to be a girl. All I knew is that whenever I stepped into an Abercrombie I felt like a cat burglar frozen in a police spotlight. The jig was up.

Then again, I might have been overthinking things. The problem was in a way, right behind me.

In a word, ass. I had one, suddenly. Did my butt cross the threshold one night as I slept, silent as the plague? Maybe I was just not paying attention as it expanded steadily as an inflated soccer ball until there it was, bouncing in time with each step, inescapable as my shadow. My ass did not match the rest of my body. It was just *there*, jutting from above my scrawny legs like a knot in a tree branch, imbalanced and humiliating and a real frickin' problem. At the end of the day the elastic on my Fruit of the Loom underwear had cut purple lines in my pale hips. I would catch my reflection in a dark window and feel like I was merely operating a body that didn't belong to me. For the first time, I began to weigh myself. No matter that I was playing the best soccer of my life. That winter I joined the high school track team to stay in shape and ran a 5:38 mile, collapsing at the finish line in disbelief at what I was capable of. The moment I grew into the power of my body I was learning to hate it and how fucked is that?

I did not buy my first piece of Abercrombie clothing at Abercrombie. Instead, I dug up a few pairs of jeans at T.J. Maxx, the labels scribbled over with black marker which made me suspect that on their journey to the North Haven strip mall they'd fallen off the back of a truck. My mom paid for pairs in light and dark wash, both low-rise, and while not fitting me, they were close enough, their belt loops just reaching my tailbone. They were stiff, they had useless pockets, they shrunk in the wash. I wore them every day.

I had finally bent the knee to Michael Jeffries (figuratively, of course, you're not able to bend your knees in pants that tight), and now my school outfits consisted of bootcut Abercrombie jeans, Day-Glo Chuck Taylors, and a tank top I'd forcefully tuck in to prevent my butt cheeks from popping out of my pants like bread from a toaster. As an added precaution, I sat in the back row of the classroom, never bent down to retie my shoes, and stopped running after the bus, no matter how late I was. When I got home from school I'd tune into the afternoon *Law & Order* block on TNT and leave my jeans in a pile on the kitchen floor. I became obsessed with that small gesture Jack McCoy and the other male lawyers made, neatly tugging up the legs of their trousers to give the fabric slack before they settled into their chairs. What luxury, to adjust your pants to your body as opposed to the other way around. No wonder the girls of my generation were enthralled by a novel about a pair of jeans that magically fit every member of a friend group.

McQueen also hated how he looked. He was too fat, too oikish, and in the fashion world, was never allowed to forget it. "His slightly soiled shirt open at the neck; the chic way he carries a can of beer; and that haircut 'très football-club de Liverpool,'" sneered a French magazine. "Compared with him, an audience of AC/DC heavy-metal fans would win prizes for couture." He was called *éléphant terrible*, a boiled sausage, yobbo, "malevolent Edward Scissorhands." *Vanity Fair* took note of McQueen's "dome of belly visible under his sweater, and little button eyes set atop huge Muppety cheeks," and a reporter for *Details* magazine wrote that with McQueen's "blue eyes, downy puffs of facial hair, and an overbite flashing out of a narrow mouth, he resembles a walrus." A friend of McQueen's told biographer Andrew Wilson, "There is this tyranny of people, like Tom Ford, who really work on their look… Poor Lee would have thought, 'I'm in a glamorous world, but…'" In an interview with David Bowie for *Dazed & Confused*, McQueen said, "I can't cure the world of illness with clothes. I just try to make the person that's wearing them feel more confident in themselves because I am so unconfident."

McQueen's social life further pushed him outside the bounds of good taste. He boozed, stole, started food fights in nice restaurants. He'd greet his friends at the pub by sticking a finger up his ass and thrusting it under their noses. He felt a deep personal affinity with the Marquis de Sade. "He was an unashamed hedonist," writes Wilson. "He adored both the finest caviar and a treat of beans and poached eggs on toast while sitting on the sofa... He loved Maker's Mark and Diet Coke, the sleazier end of gay pornography and a great deal of anonymous sex." Some habits he never outgrew. "He made a lot of drug dealers rich," said an ex-boyfriend. "He could do three [clothing] collections in a day and a half with cocaine—it opened something up in him. But it also took a piece of him away, and with that came the paranoia." McQueen's romantic relationships were volatile. As an employer, he'd veer from supportive to exploitative and back until the staff member resigned, at which point McQueen would never speak to them again. "There was the sober him, an insecure, unhappy person," remembers a friend. "Then there was this intermediate one, this brilliant genius who was escaping with the aid of alcohol and drugs; and then this drunken jerk that went into a state of psychotic weirdness that I did not understand."

McQueen was publicly beloved for his pugnacity—he refused to apologize after chucking a baked potato at Madonna's head at a dinner party, saying she was too "stuck up her own backside to worry about anyone else"—but if he wanted to satisfy his career ambitions, he'd need to sand down the edges that made him famous in the first place. "Designers like Ralph Lauren and Calvin Klein are all about looking good, and for them it is just as much about marketing themselves as marketing of the clothes," said a friend. Jeffries may have given all of himself to Ab-

ercrombie, but there was zero separation between Mc-
Queen the person, the brand, and the designs. With every
success—and McQueen was becoming one of the most
successful designers of all time—he only felt more pres-
sure to sell the work by changing himself.

Eventually McQueen got his teeth fixed and dyed his
hair blond. He saw a personal trainer for a while, but
was doing so much cocaine the trainer grew concerned
he'd have a heart attack while working out. He took di-
etary supplements. He got liposuction but claimed it was
crap and didn't work for men. After gastric band surgery
he lost a lot of weight very fast. The same industry that
called McQueen a walrus gushed over his new figure.
"As well as pioneering trends to direct each fashion season, Alexander McQueen could also stand up as a lu-
minary of the diet world," wrote *British Vogue* in 2003,
describing the designer as a "noticeably slimmer, firmer
version of the chubby bad boy of old." When the Coun-
cil of Fashion Designers in America named McQueen
Best International Designer, Kate Moss made sure to
note his thinness in the ceremony brochure. For a while
at least, McQueen was stoked about his changed body.
"It's more to do with wanting to look in the mirror and
think, 'God, I really fancy you,'" he told *Vogue*. But
friends barely recognized him. "He was trying to con-
form, live up to a celebrity status, and it just didn't suit
him," said an ex. "He was half the size I remember him,
really pale and lost," said Sebastian Pons, McQueen's former assistant, remembering that post-op, McQueen "had

the physique but couldn't take his top off. Now what he didn't want to show was the scar."

If it's not clear by now, bad things happen when you take your fashion cues from girls who fly private. When I wasn't playing soccer with the daughters of hedge fund managers, I attended Wilbur Cross High School, where the most popular kid in school was a junior named Desiree who was as big and strong as our starting linebacker and voted homecoming queen. Popularity, hierarchies, it just worked differently than the schools on TV. There were metal detectors and a daycare in the basement so kids could drop off their babies and stay in class. Military recruiters sniffed around the hallways and the city police would show up to diligently maintain the school to prison pipeline. Sometimes a celebrity would visit for "straight talk," like when Michael Vick came to tell us not to do dog fighting.

What I'm saying is, I didn't go to Abercrombie High. The student body was mostly Black, Puerto Rican, and Mexican, with Asian and white kids rounding out the population of fifteen hundred. As far as a unified style exists in a population of that size, most of my classmates dressed in streetwear, which unlike my new predistressed jeans, they kept fresh and clean. There weren't many frayed hems at Wilbur Cross. The guys kept the holographic stickers on the brims of their hats and carried brushes to spruce up their Timbs. As far as brands went, there was a lot of Puma and Adidas, companies like Diesel, Rocawear, Ecko, Baby Phat. But your popularity didn't depend on the tags on your clothes. Desiree wore a cheap

tank top and white leggings to school every day. When
Flo Rida's "Low" came out, instead of buying Apple Bottoms jeans the girls just airbrushed Granny Smiths onto
the back pockets of their off-brand cotton shorts.

The overt bullying, such that it was, came from the
adult administrators. Assistant principals passed out
three-day suspensions for anyone wearing a baseball cap
or winter coat in the hallway, or if your jeans sagged too
low, which had become a full-blown American moral
panic. (During that time, multiple cities criminalized
low-hanging pants under the racist claim the style pro-
moted gang culture. In Shreveport, thirty-one-year-
old Anthony Childs was stopped by police for his saggy
jeans, and when he fled he was shot three times in the
back and killed.) At Wilbur Cross, "pull your pants up"
was a constant refrain. It was shouted at my male classmates by teachers, guidance counselors, security guards.
And every other month or so we'd get herded into the
auditorium, where another motivational speaker would
yell at us about self-respect.

The thing was, no one taught me more about self-
respect than the kids at my high school, certainly not my
Fairfield County soccer teammates or the good people
at Abercrombie. As I made new friends, saw which girls
were idolized and what was in style, a lightbulb flick-
ered above my dumb white head. Could it be that there
existed whole swaths of people for whom a fat ass wasn't
a punchline but something to value? I found body posi-
tivity wherever white people weren't—my high school,
in the pocket. There was "My Humps," "Bootylicious,"

Ghostface Killah's "Tush" where Missy Elliot raps, "you seem real determined to put a hurtin' / But if you ain't slurpin', then you better off jerkin'"—oh, how much better life would have been if at that impressionable age I had listened to more Missy Elliot! My younger sister and I loved "Baby Got Back" and watched the video constantly, that is until our dad, bless him, put a stop to it, on the grounds that it was demeaning to women. How could I explain that the line "my anaconda don't want none unless you've got buns, hun" was actually a terrific piece of news for a girl growing up in a world of Paris Hilton and *Shallow Hal*, where white women took to the pages of the *Washington Post* to complain that their StairMasters made their butts too big.

But let's not kid ourselves. Sir Mix-a-Lot was singing about women who looked like Flo Jo, and if I had any place in that song, it was as one of the white girls in the prelude—"I mean, her *butt*, it's just so big... I can't believe it's just so *round*... She's just so, *Black*." And I was just so white. The girls on the track team valiantly tried to teach me to dance, but that just ended with me bent at the waist in the gymnasium while they shouted, "Shake your ass, Natalie!" We all know I'd look like a mess in air-brushed jeans, and if I had tried to copy the Black girls in my life instead of the white ones, I'd be in a different kind of trouble. I knew my place. For a while longer, I kept buying what Jeffries was selling.

Under Jeffries, Abercrombie was a particularly racist brand. The employee handbook forbade Black hairstyles.

Weber's imagery almost exclusively celebrated whiteness. The company was sued for discriminatory hiring practices, and argued in court that they fired their employees of color not because they weren't white, but because they were ugly. (Abercrombie settled the lawsuit while admitting no guilt.) Stores sold shirts featuring gross Asian and Latinx stereotypes and kept selling them, even when picketed and boycotted. Why? "The kids—the consumers—just loved wearing those tees," a former Abercrombie merchandiser admitted in the 2022 documentary *White Hot*. "So we kept making them. And they were cheap. You could sell the tees for like an 85% markup." Jeffries too defended the bigotry as a savvy brand strategy. "Those companies that are in trouble are trying to target everybody: young, old, fat, skinny. But then you become totally vanilla," he told *Salon* in that interview that will be mentioned in his obituary. "You don't alienate anybody, but you don't excite anybody, either."

The racist slogans, the women's shirts that read "Who needs a brain when you have these?", the thongs for little girls, the brand's public refusal to sell plus sizes, were not just in poor taste but a test: Are you one of them or one of us?

Meanwhile, disordered eating was suddenly everywhere in my life like a stomach bug going around. Close friends were binging and purging. Teammates opted for garden salads at carbo-loading dinners. There was calorie counting, cutting, obsessive exercising, the word *thinspiration* was thrown around. Karen Carpenter, who died from anorexia in 1983, grew up in New Haven, just a

couple blocks away from my childhood soccer field and
now some of the girls I played with back then, once
strong and intimidating, were easily pushed off the ball.
My coaches kicked the grass in exasperation and sent
them to the bench. There were rumors that a few older
players were too skinny to get cleared to play by their
college doctors, cautionary tales to get our shit together.
My sophomore and junior years were booked with show-
case tournaments around the country, our chance to
win a spot on a top college team, but for many of my
teammates, it became impossible to reconcile the body
of a top soccer player and that of a good-looking girl. In
training, we pushed ourselves to become muscular and
immovable. Off the field, the perfect body had anemia
and a thigh gap.

Adolescence is, to borrow from poet Trish Low, a
chronic matter of wanting, of forcing desire, despite itself,
into a shape, and in my case, the shape was made out of distressed denim. I began to wonder if it had to be that way.

When I turned sixteen I opted out. I had tried to wear
my Abercrombie jeans and foam flip-flops and a horri-
ble miniskirt that twisted backward around my waist as I
walked. I had straightened my hair and shaved my legs, and
in the mornings put on my foundation and mascara, but
who was I fooling? I'd say I hated myself, but I didn't even
know who I was. In tenth grade, I said, "fuck it." That year
I exclusively wore flannel pajama bottoms to school. I no
longer bothered to brush my hair before scraping it into a
ponytail. Bedroom slippers rounded out the ensemble, with
a novelty mail-order sweatshirt for Beach University (my

safety school, I told people). When it got cold I accessorized with a ratty gray hat I claimed I'd found in the gutter. That was self-mythologizing—the hat actually came from the back of my dad's closet—but it was my way of claiming my rightful place as the butt of the joke. My teammates made fun of me because I was begging them to. I remembered the lesson I learned from hide-and-seek years before: when you're destined to lose, the worst thing you can do is still try. I was done attempting to look cute and failing at it. There was no way I was getting back under the Audi.

Secretly, I liked the way I looked in sweats and slippers. I looked like shit, but when I caught my reflection I saw a girl with better things to think about than outfits. By disengaging, I thought I could get back to my old life, when I only wore soccer shorts and my friends weren't running to the bathroom after meals, when my body was a teammate instead of my opponent, and I could still play pickup with the boys after school. As for my crushes, I assumed that my new look wouldn't affect my dating plans. I told myself that the boys I liked knew I was a chill hang and an All-State athlete, all of which would of course make up for my bedraggled appearance. In my entire life, I have never been more wrong.

I was wearing a vintage Batman sweatshirt and watching *The Fugitive* when I finally had my first kiss. He tugged at my sleeve and said, "Can Batman take a break?" The thrill of my young life! Soon after, he ghosted me (a complex maneuver when you have classes together), and I was left casting about for reasons why. It had to be my appearance, I concluded, which I must stress, was slovenly. There was a reason I had plenty of friends but no reciprocated romantic interest. I couldn't refuse to play the game, I realized, not if I wanted to be wanted. No one dreams of making out with an androgynous pile of laundry. It's famously gender, and not soccer, that's the extent we go to in order to be loved.

The autumn high school season made way for winter college showcases in Orlando and Las Vegas and then summer training camps held on empty campuses, cycles of tryouts, fitness tests, recruitment, letters of intent. In ninety-minute increments my life moved forward. By the end of high school everyone on CFC hated each other, which is why we were never as dominant as we could have been. We split into factions, mostly down class lines, and I stood even further outside, just me and two friends from the greater New Haven area. By that point I knew that just because we played on the same team didn't mean we needed to be the same people.

At tryouts for my university team, those of us with thick thighs and asses made the cut, while the skinny players, no matter how skillful, were often muscled out. Of my new teammates, only a few of them could fit into low-rise jeans, not that they would even have wanted to.

By the 2010s, the trend had died. It was a time of fast fashion and internet shopping, where the shock and awe of the Abercrombie retail experience had no sway on virtual consumers. Bigotry is a good brand strategy until it isn't. Abercrombie became associated with bullies and racists, kids who peaked in high school. Times had changed. Our president was Black, Beyoncé was a feminist and feminism was a brand, and racism became, at the very least, no longer a savvy way to sell T-shirts. Gwyneth Paltrow grew back her pubic hair. Kim Kardashian broke the internet. Social media became one infinite banner ad for Brazilian butt lifts. *Twerk* was added to *The Oxford English Dictionary.* My favorite coach pleaded guilty in the Varsity Blues scandal for selling a spot on the Yale soccer team. My least favorite coach was fired after he texted a thirteen-year-old player "I can't stop thinking of you." Bruce Weber was accused by multiple models of sexual assault. (Allegations he denies.) Abercrombie owner Les Wexner came under scrutiny when we learned his best friend was Jeffrey Epstein. Abercrombie's stock plummeted.

And the rise of our pants, as if tied to sea levels, kept going up. Levi's released Ribcage jeans with a twelve-and-an-eighth-inch rise, while Madewell, Reformation, and Topshop all sold versions explicitly advertised as mom jeans. "Personally, I want my pants to be so high that they double as an underwire bra," wrote Rachel Syme for the *New Yorker* in 2019. "High-rise pants put us in a direct, friendly confrontation with our proportions. Perhaps women are less afraid to have that interaction now, or perhaps we've just grown tired of draping ourselves in euphemism."

Alexander McQueen became one of the most successful and admired designers of all time, and then began to talk about himself in the past tense. "Anger in my work reflected angst in my personal life. What people see is me coming to terms with what I was in life," he told fashion editor Suzy Menkes. He told another friend he planned on killing himself as part of his final show. He'd appear on stage, he said, inside a clear box and shoot himself in the head, so the audience could see his blood drip down the glass walls. One last *fuck off* to the establishment. Or maybe a final act of metamorphosis, turning anguish into spectacle, glamor even. McQueen "yearned for a place, a state, an idea, a man, a dress, a dream, a drug that would transform his reality," wrote his biographer. "Ultimately he was addicted to the lure of fantasy, the prospect that one day he might be free of his body, his memories, his regrets, his past."

In February 2010, McQueen's mother died after a long illness, and nine days later, the designer ended his own life in private. He was buried on the Isle of Skye, his tombstone inscribed with the same words from *A Midsummer Night's Dream* that were tattooed on his arm: "Love looks not with the eyes but with the mind." Before, when asked by a reporter about the future of fashion, McQueen said he'd like to forge a dress out of liquid steel. "I can't, because it'd scald the person wearing it," he said. "Someone's got to live, or what's the point?"

Michael Jeffries hung on at Abercrombie through plummeting stock prices and accumulating lawsuits. He turned the music down and reduced the amount of cologne sprayed in the store by 25 percent. The moose logo shrunk, prices lowered, Ruehl No.925 was wiped from existence, and Jeffries began to consider carrying plus sizes. But when you've spent two obsessive decades building a brand identity, it's not the kind of thing you can easily change. ("Like taking a dinosaur out of the sea," McQueen once said about rebranding.) "Mike indelibly linked his entire persona, his soul, to the brand's image," remarked one retail consultant. "For him to change the brand would have taken the greatest psychologist in the world."

If the company was still making money no one would have cared about his obscene CEO salary or the discrimination lawsuits, but as any teenager could tell you, the popular group isn't known for loyalty. In 2014, the board forced Jeffries into retirement. He hasn't been seen in public life since.

As for me, I played soccer until I busted my knee at the start of my senior year of college. The surgeon needed to remove 60 percent of my meniscus, and I haven't been able to play since. When I'm in a mood, I say to my husband, "You don't even know me."

"Sure I do!" he says.

"Impossible," I tell him, "because you've never seen me play soccer," and he throws up his hands and walks to the other side of the living room, grumbling about jocks.

These days when I wear jeans they're high-waisted, but lately I've gravitated toward coveralls and jumpsuits, and have a closet full of them. I wonder if this is because they're comfortably androgynous, or if, as always, I'm just happier in a uniform. I've begun to wonder the same thing about my name. My whole life I've preferred Nat over Natalie, the latter I associate with drowning in a nightgown off Catalina Island. Nat was what my friends and teammates called me, and it's also the name chosen by someone backing slowly away from their gender, the way you might react to a raccoon acting weird in the daytime.

This isn't me coming out, as the only thing I'm coming out of is a breathtakingly uncomfortable pair of pants. (That said, many of the former homophobes I played with now have girlfriends.) For most of my life I assumed I didn't feel like a girl because I was lousy at femininity, that I somehow missed the sleepover where everyone learned how to apply eyeliner. Now I'm not so sure. The whole female gender seems predetermined by an R & D department. Like a girl is someone who shoplifted herself.

In any event, I can now recognize that I never fit into Abercrombie jeans not because I was uniquely misshapen, but because *no one* fits into Abercrombie jeans. Not covering your ass was the entire point. I wish I could say that this revelation came to me in a lightning bolt of self-worth. In reality, hating the way I looked just got too boring. Seriously, apart from the merchandise at Abercrombie, is there anything more tedious than self-loathing? It's like riding the bench in your own life. Gender, soccer, clothing, they're all just a game to play, and you only run into trouble when the game plays you. "People forget that fashion is about showing who you are," said McQueen.

When I think about being thirteen, fourteen, that age when, for better or worse, your body is growing out to meet the world, I think about playing soccer in the rain. The rich smell of wet leather and pulped grass. Steam rising off our skin. Water spraying from our ponytails. I think of sliding belly-first through the mud with my team, shrieking. Our uniforms are so drenched they're almost falling off us. At home, my low-rise jeans are buried away in my dresser.

Back then I took it as a failure, even a character defect, that I couldn't comfortably fit in my clothes. What if instead I had decided this wasn't a crisis, but a sign of exuberance and unbridledness? "Beauty is not a luxury," writes Saidiya Hartman, "rather it is a way of creating possibility in the space of enclosure." Maybe that's what I meant when I wrote in my high school diary, "I don't care about being beautiful. I just want to be beautiful enough to be loved."

When Christie's auctioned off Princess Diana's wardrobe, they turned the garments inside out and discovered hidden second dresses built into the structure. "The dresses stood up and almost walked," observed Hilary Mantel. "After her death, they alone retained the shape of the princess." And if someone got their hands on my teenage clothes, what shape would they reveal? Choose either the distressed low-rise jeans or the soccer uniform muddied and soaked through. Either way I think, you'd find that the clothes failed to contain the girl inside them like a defender caught flat-footed. Which would put me on a breakaway—the field open before me, my legs devouring space, my team at my back, the ball at my feet, not a girl but a soccer girl, taking the game in stride.

SELF-CENTERED

When I was a sophomore in college, I took a creative nonfiction workshop and met a girl who was everything I wasn't. The point of the class was to learn to write your own story, but from the moment we met I focused instead on helping her tell her own, first in notes after workshop, then later editing her Instagram captions and cowriting a book proposal she sold for hundreds of thousands of dollars. It seems obvious now, the way the story would end, but when I first met Caroline Calloway, all I saw was the beginning of something extraordinary.

Today Caroline is a twenty-seven-year-old Instagram influencer with almost eight hundred thousand followers.

A self-described "writer, art historian, and teacher," she first became internet famous for diaristic captions chronicling her misadventures as an American undergrad at Cambridge University and was later known for the mysterious dissolution of her big book deal. After that, Caroline fell out of the public eye for a year but returned this past January on a tour to promote her Creativity Workshop, which was billed as a tutorial to "architect a life that feels really full and genuine and rich and beautiful" but ended up being compared to a one-woman Fyre Fest. She charged participants $165 a head and sold the tickets before booking venues, made promises she couldn't deliver on (orchid crowns, "cooked" salad), and, true to form, posted the whole fiasco in real time. It seemed like the entire internet saw a pallet of twelve hundred Mason jars delivered to her studio apartment where she had no place to store them, and her pleas for ticket buyers to the canceled Philly event to just take the train to New York. She became a symbol of, as journalist Kayleigh Donaldson put it, "The Empty Mason Jar of the Influencer Economy," which prompted Caroline to begin selling T-shirts that read Stop Hate Following Me, Kayleigh.

More recently, her Instagram has been filled with emotional posts about this very essay, which she knew was coming. For almost a week she's been posting constantly—how much she misses our friendship, how hurt and ashamed she is about whatever she thinks I'll say here, how relieved she is that I broke the trust in our relationship so she can now write about me, too. It's been surreal watching this unfold from my desk job in Los Angeles, but I'm not surprised she's taken an essay of mine that didn't exist yet and turned it into a narrative for herself. Caroline was the most confident girl I'd ever known. We were both twenty-year-old NYU students when we met, Caroline arriving late to the first day of class, wearing a designer dress, not knowing who Lorrie Moore was but claiming she could recite the poems of Catullus in Latin. She had silk eyelashes and wore cashmere sweaters without a bra, and for class she turned in personal essays about heartbreak and boarding school. She seemed like an adult, someone who had just gone ahead and constructed a life of independence. I, meanwhile, was a virgin with a meek ponytail, living in a railroad apartment that was sinking into the Gowanus Canal.

Caroline first took an interest in me after I wrote an essay about growing up in New Haven. Yale was an obsession of hers; she'd been rejected and never got over it. The fact that I was a Yale townie won me an invitation to her West Village apartment, a studio painted Tiffany Blue and filled with fresh orchids and hardcovers. "This is my Yale box," she told me, sitting me on her white loveseat and showing me a shoe box of Handsome Dan and Beinecke Library memorabilia. It was that same day, as we split a joint, that Caroline informed me I was beautiful, which no one outside my family had ever said. Soon I began going to Caroline's after every class, then just any chance I could. To my other friends, I described her as someone you couldn't count on to remember a birthday, but the one I'd call if I needed a black-market kidney. What I meant was that she was someone to write about, and that was what I wanted most of all. "You're a sharp writer," our professor had told me—he would soon be played by Jesse Eisenberg in a movie, and Caroline and I were both a little obsessed—"but what you're limited by right now is where you've walked through yourself—you're limited by your itinerary."

Caroline had no such limits. Her life was a cycle of adventures and minor crises. We dashed in and out of as many clubs as we could in a night, attended a *Wet Hot American Summer*–themed party at a secret society, and went to *Cyrano de Bergerac* on Broadway, which Caroline wept through as if it was a religious experience. We'd go out to eat all the time, and soon I was broke but didn't care. I was now part of her life, a conspirator and confidante.

At the Minetta Tavern, I told her that her fantasy of going out with our professor was dangerous and predictable.

"It's like a movie," I said between bites of pork belly. "This is Act I. Soon he'll invite you over to his bachelor pad, fuck you, and in five months you'll read all about it in the *New Yorker*."

"Go on," she said. "What happens to me next?"

For the next two hours, I ad-libbed the movie of her life, and she paid for my meal. "You're a genius," she said, and I had no reason to question her.

That December, for her twenty-first birthday, I gave Caroline a gift: three dinner plates stamped with the Yale crest that my mom had found outside a campus building. I took a Sharpie and wrote "Fuck It" on their backs. When Caroline unwrapped them, she broke into tears. Real tears. I paused. *Was this really that excellent of a gift? Had she never received something stupid and personal before?* Which is why I was surprised when later that winter she informed me that the Yale plates had been stolen from her apartment. Her tone was nonchalant. "What do you mean they were stolen?" I remember asking. "They're worthless, and you live in an apartment filled with Apple products and antique furniture." She told me that it wasn't just the plates and insisted that her Exeter ring had been stolen, too. It just didn't make sense. Who would steal a bunch of used plates scrawled with permanent marker? It was the first time I felt sure she was lying to me. But I didn't call her on it. What was I going to do, torch everything we had over a gag gift? And if she was lying about the stolen plates, then maybe she was lying about the extent of our friendship or me being a beautiful genius. Even a few weeks later, when I saw her once again wearing her Exeter ring, I didn't say anything. It was easier to listen to her talk as we strolled through the West Village, past the Waverley Inn, where she made me promise we'd go together when we officially *made it.*

A year after Caroline and I met, the world was introduced to Caroline Calloway the influencer. That spring, at the end of my semester abroad in London, Caroline flew out to travel to Sicily with me. When she arrived, she told me she was getting more active on this new platform called Instagram. Apparently she had posted a color wheel of macarons that had landed on the "favorites page," and now she had fifty thousand followers, mostly teen girls who wanted a life like hers. Caroline had always been obsessive and confident, but Instagram focused those qualities like sunlight through a magnifying glass.

Her account was called #Adventuregrams. "You can have an adventure anywhere, if you're curious," she told me as I took pictures of her balancing on a stone wall. "That's what the brand is about. It doesn't matter where you live or how much money you have. You could be a teen from Nebraska and by following me you can feel like you're here." But I was the one who was actually there, standing right next to her, and already I was beginning to feel invisible. When we left our room in the morning, she packed several outfits so she could pose for days' worth of photos in one afternoon. I was deputized as the photographer, instructed to find her best angles and keep my shadow out of the frame. When Caroline was satisfied we got the shot, we'd hurry back to the hotel to connect to the Wi-Fi, brainstorming the caption together. After she posted the photo, she would hold her phone in her palm and watch as the comments rolled in, responding to each one. She was building a second version of herself in front of me, and how could I compete with that? I should have been having the time of my life in paradise, but Caroline had a way of making me feel small, as if I had folded myself up like a travel toothbrush so she could take me along for the trip.

For a long time, though, the way I remembered this vacation was through the photos she posted. The sea glass and cave exploring, the pizza we ate at what Caroline mistranslated as "The Fountain of Female Shame." And then there was the single best picture ever taken of me: at the summit of the volcano, steam billows behind me and I'm adjusting my sunglasses (which belonged to Caroline). I never felt better than when viewed through Caroline's eyes. But a year later, I came across the journal I'd kept on the trip and realized how bitter I'd been. "I found myself wishing something bad would happen...a humiliation, like the one I feel always," I had written. "There has to be a price for getting everything you want. For never being embarrassed." It read like a tantrum: "I am beginning to feel like a child or an unpaid intern," I wrote, "both of which I had been recently and never wanted to be again."

The trip had bigger problems, though. As we tried to make our way out of Italy, we missed three nonrefundable flights because of heavy wind. I was now officially broke and didn't know how I'd afford to get home. Caroline saved the day. She spoke the language, pretty-cried in front of airport staff, and sat cross-legged on the floor of the Milan airport with her parents' credit cards fanned in front of her. "I don't know how I'm going to be able to pay you back," I said. "These flights cost more than my rent." She waved off my concerns and we parted ways, me back to my parents' house in New Haven, Caroline on to her next adventure in Venice.

I was the one who offered to spend the summer editing Caroline's Instagram posts to pay her back. I was making $10 an hour working at a recycling center/prop shop in Gowanus, and my new roommate, a male model, had bought a pet bunny but had stopped paying rent. I was barely holding my life together. Working off the $800 or so I owed Caroline was the only plan I had. Besides, there was something I liked about being bound closer to her, forced to stay in her life through our arrangement.

For the three months I helped develop #Adventure-grams, Caroline in northern Italy, me in South Brooklyn. We ran up our families' phone bills but kept gaining followers. Our captions were mostly chirpy travelogues— "Hand-made spaghetti tossed with black truffle butter and Atlantic squid ink... It's how Venetian aristocrats do munchies," "That jolt of disorientation when you wake up in a place you've never been before... And you see a sword." Watching the likes accumulate, I began to believe that what we were making mattered to my career (for the first time I was being paid to write) and to our readers around the world. It was 2013, and the internet felt like the future of writing, at least for girls. The boys from our classes were churning out different versions of *Fear and Loathing in Bushwick*, but I believed Caroline and I were busting open the form of nonfiction. *Instagram is memoir in real time. It's memoir without the act of remembering. It's collapsing the distance between writer and reader and critic, which is why it's true feminist storytelling*, I'd argue to Caroline, trying to convince her that a white girl learning to believe in herself could be the height of radicalism (convenient, as I too was a white girl learning to believe in herself).

Our arrangement came to an end as the summer did. I returned to NYU for my final semester, and Caroline flew to Cambridge University to restart her first. (She always claimed she couldn't bear to go through life with

an NYU-alumni email address.) That fall, things in the
Gowanus apartment deteriorated. My roommate still
wasn't paying the rent, his rabbit ate black paint left on
the floor and dropped dead, we got bedbugs, and our
landlord wanted us out. Caroline's West Village studio
was sitting unoccupied, so I asked if I could sublet for a
few months for a reduced rate in exchange for working
on captions. Caroline agreed. But a week before I was
supposed to move in, she called with a change of plans,
something about the value of gold having dropped and
her family being low on money. Now she had to rent
the apartment on Airbnb and needed me as the super—
greet the guests, clean the bedding. She would pay me
$200 a week, which, she assured me, would be more
than enough to rent some other place.

My first day on the job, I let myself into the studio
to tidy up before the guests arrived. There was a bag of
months-old trash on the kitchen floor, and Caroline's
white comforter was stained. I balled the comforter up,
stuffed it under the bed, and sank to the ground. The
night before, I had been on a date with an older man. He
bought me a few drinks and took me back to his place
in Bay Ridge, where he called me a whore and hit and
choked me in bed. That morning, on the way to Caroline's, he texted me, "I hope your chest isn't still sticky." It
was only the second time I'd had sex, and all I wanted was
to figure out how to make it an anecdote to laugh about,
an experience that would make me interesting. I wanted
to be a cool Brooklyn girl about it, but I kept thinking
about how, on Caroline's first day at Cambridge, she met

a handsome Swede who filled her room with flowers and was entirely devoted to her. If I were more like Caroline, I thought, more beautiful and fun, if I radiated girlishness, then men would view me as someone worthy of care. I would have my own midnight adventures with Italian gentlemen, my life so enviable that my only job would be living it to its fullest. Instead, that morning I had to chew my egg sandwich on the side of my mouth that hadn't been hit, and now I was cleaning an apartment I'd never live in, belonging to a girl I could never be.

"Caroline, I don't want to be your maid," I told her the next day over Skype. "I'm sorry I can't help you out, but can you ask someone else?"

"Oh no, Natalie, I would," she said, her new boyfriend sitting supportively next to her. "It's just, you're the only one of my friends who needs the money badly enough to take the job."

As a recent graduate and without a place to live, I moved back in with my parents. "That Caroline girl is bad news," my mom kept telling me, echoing what all my friends had been saying since I came back from Sicily. "Yeah, no shit," I'd reply. It wasn't as if I didn't know Caroline would always let me down; after all, no one knew her better than I did.

Meanwhile, Caroline continued to post daily from Cambridge without my help, growing her fan base internationally and making new, posh friends. I submitted captions we had written together as work samples to corporate social media positions but never heard back; I placed #Adventuregrams at the top of my résumé, describing myself as an editor, or if the listing called for it, the "personal assistant to Ms. Calloway." I eventually put my BFA to good use, finding work painting apartments, editing college essays, and packaging Urban Outfitters jewelry in a Chinatown warehouse between a funeral home and fish market. A couple friends and I found a Sunset Park apartment filled with natural light and German cockroaches, and I settled into a postgrad existence that I hoped was more than just making rent, but somehow added up to a writer's life.

In the spring of 2015, I began receiving texts from friends and family along the lines of "Have you seen this Caroline story?" and "Is your Instagram friend like actually famous now?" Apparently, she was on a press tour, written about in the *Daily Mail* and *Mic*. She had an agent, Byrd Leavell (who also represented the Fat Jewish, Cat Marnell, and soon the author of *Crippled America*, Donald Trump). It was my greatest fear: Caroline was leaving me behind. It had been ages since we last spoke, and even longer since I'd written with her, but I reached back out.

You must be so happy, what with 90,000 followers and counting... I feel strange being an excited onlooker, I emailed her.

Receiving no response, I emailed again. Wanna bounce ideas off me? Let me know! I'm here for you!

YO get back to me, girl. I just wanna check in and be your ally and do some planning!

That September, I finally got the call. Caroline was back in New York, her book proposal was due after the weekend, and she needed my help. I grabbed my toothbrush and headed up to her apartment to get to work.

We fit right back into our roles: the protagonist and the punch-up writer. We wrote giddily through the night, our laptops burning into our thighs. We banged out dozens of pages—Caroline's New York–Sweden love triangle, befriending European noblemen at midnight at the Piazza San Marco. We were high off our asses on working together again and being twenty-three, and also Adderall, which Caroline paid cash for from a doctor near Washington Square Park whose waiting room was exclusively homeless men and NYU girls in Lululemon. By sunrise, cracked-open pill capsules rolled across the coffee table and we smoked joints to be hungry enough to eat the burritos we ordered. Around hour forty, Caroline turned to me and officially asked me to come on as a paid editor. I was so tired I was hallucinating the tools I had used at my landscaping job the Friday we began. A chainsaw and garden spade floated above Caroline's head as she asked me what a fair percentage was, and I blearily suggested thirty-five. She agreed.

I woke up next to Caroline in her big fluffy bed. Nothing we wrote that night was usable, and the life-changing deal Caroline and I had struck was legally nothing more than a stoned handshake. But it was still real to us, and I got right to work. She'd blown her first deadline, but we decided to keep working until it was done. For the next two months, I'd wake up at 6:00 a.m. in Sunset Park and write for ninety minutes, usually working off raw notes Caroline sent over for the chapter we were on. I'd craft it into a legible narrative and then rush to my landscaping job where, from 8:00 a.m. to 4:00 p.m., I'd install tasteful fences and patios for the gentrifiers of Bed-Stuy and Prospect Heights, while Caroline filled in the details. On nights and weekends, we'd meet, always at Caroline's (my apartment made her too sad, she told me). Caroline loved to read our pages aloud, and I loved to listen. What all the think pieces this year missed was the power of her voice, syrupy and sincere, persuasive to the point that when she read our drafts, I couldn't trust my ability to know what was great and what just sounded that way coming out of her mouth. But when we finally finished the 103-page proposal, I was sure it was good. The Caroline character we created together was a fantastic YA protagonist; she loved and was loved, looked good crying, stomped around an idealized New York in her I-deserve-to-be-here boots.

"The talent you show in this proposal, both in the writing and the photos from the entire story is this rare, remarkable thing," Byrd emailed. It was a proposal for a memoir of a life that wasn't mine, adapted from Instagram captions, and I was proud.

The proposal was originally called *School Girl* (my suggestion) but Caroline deemed that too pornographic, so went with her first choice, *And We Were Like*, as in the way girls begin to tell stories. The first week of November, Caroline and Byrd took the proposal out to publishing houses while I waited for updates. The good news rolled in—the executives loved the writing, loved Caro-

line. My involvement was uncredited, as the entire selling point of Caroline was that she was an ingénue, and
ingénues don't have sleep-deprived collaborators living
in deep Brooklyn. I knew my job was to be present but
invisible, but it still hurt to hear secondhand about the
high-powered meetings, the gushing over pages I half
wrote. But how could I complain? In the end, Flatiron
agreed to pay $375,000 for the book, some of which
would be mine.

Caroline and I kept our promise and celebrated at the
Waverley Inn. We ordered the New York strip and truffle mac and cheese, got drunk off manhattans and a bottle of champagne. A table of Wall Street guys sent over
tequila shots, and at the end of the meal, I excused myself
and went over. "Hey, so which one of you sent over the
drink?" I asked. They all wore oxford shirts with those
Gordon Gekko white collars and cuffs. None of them
said anything. "Well, here's my number, for whoever it
was." I passed over a piece of notebook paper with my
cell, and when I turned around, they broke into laughter.
I went back to our table, but Caroline was gone. I waited,
but she didn't return. I checked the bathroom and wan-
dered the restaurant holding our glasses of champagne.
Finally she answered her cell phone. She had gone to
meet up with Byrd, she said, and I should come. I passed
the table of Wall Street guys to get her genuine-leopard-
skin coat she'd forgotten, and then I walked unsteadily
into the night, trying to keep up.

In January 2016, an artist friend I connected with
Caroline to help with the book layout forwarded me

an email from Caroline that read, "Since getting back to Cambridge I've been having a really tough time and I'm not sure if I'm going to be able to finish the book at all." I didn't know why Caroline didn't tell me this, but I called her immediately. "Don't panic," I said. "I'll see you soon."

When I walked into Caroline's room in Cambridge, I saw a trash can full of daffodils beside a trash can full of Prosecco corks. She had ripped up the wall-to-wall carpet and shoved the squares into her closet because she had always wanted exposed wood floors, but you couldn't even step out of bed without getting splinters. I spent my first couple of days adjusting from jet lag and pulling shards of wood from my feet with nail clippers. But Caroline was so happy to see me I was almost taken aback. She had been so down, like everything was falling apart, she told me, but now that I was here, she felt rejuvenated and she wanted to show me everything.

Caroline lived in King's College, whose alumni include eight Nobel laureates and the inventor of the flush toilet. Students lived and went to class in stone Gothic buildings, which loomed over a great lawn that was brighter than I thought grass could be. My goal was to finish a draft in the two to three months I planned to visit, but the longer I was there, the more I saw the gap widening between the story we told and the situation on the ground. She rarely went to class, didn't hang out with friends, and hadn't started the dissertation she needed to graduate. She asked me to read the angry-professor emails she couldn't bear to and just give her the gist. One night,

I went to sleep on my air mattress while Caroline stayed at her desk buying home goods, and when I woke up the next morning, she was still hunched over eBay in her fur coat, having purchased $6,000 worth of furniture. I went to the communal bathroom and sat on the stone floor with my knees to my chest. I told myself that everyone needed furniture, and it wasn't my problem.

But Caroline's problems weren't just my problems; they were my whole world, and so while I was a supporting character in the book, I cast myself as the hero in her life. I reached out to Cambridge about therapy, spoke with her mom about her prescription pill use. When she wore the same lace gown for two and a half days, even sleeping in it, I forced her into the shower. When she arranged a loose pile of sleeping pills on her nightstand before bed, I swept them into my palm when she wasn't looking. The manuscript was due in six months, and my notes were just lists of funny British foods (Scotch eggs, juicy bits). I began to worry.

It was around this time that Caroline revealed to me that for all these years, she had been lying about her origin story. She hadn't, in fact, gotten famous from a picture of macarons on Instagram's favorites page. The real story, she told me, is she took a series of meetings with literary professionals who informed her that no one would buy a memoir from a girl with no claim to fame and no fan base. And so Caroline made one online, taking out ads designed to look like posts to promote her account and buying tens of thousands of followers. *This could ruin everything*, I thought. We had sold the proposal based on a false number; wouldn't there be consequences? If the bedrock of Caroline's Instagram account wasn't true, then was any of it? But to Caroline the ploy was a statement of intent: she was a self-made woman exploiting a new form of media. "Women spend too much time apologizing for promoting their work," she told me.

Even knowing that Caroline was the ultimate unreliable narrator, I still trusted her. After all, she was constantly calling me her best friend and work wife, telling me she loved me. I thought we were in this together. That began to change the weekend we went to Amsterdam.

The trip was ostensibly to view Van Gogh's *Almond Blossom* for Caroline's dissertation, but we ended up going out, having a few drinks, and flirting with a bartender at a tavern known for its beef stew and apple pie. When he went to refill our glasses, Caroline told me that in order to attract men, I had to allow myself to be chased, like she did with her boyfriend.

"Well, men treat you very differently than they treat me," I told her. "Look at you, look at me." I was in scuffed Timberlands and leggings under my jeans while Caroline wore a lacy baby-doll dress with knee-high suede boots. Being the foil to a hot girl was taking its toll, and writing someone else's love story was even harder. Ghostwriting for Caroline was like writing in a new tense—first person beautiful—the rules of time and inevitability were just different for her. I mean, she met a long-term boyfriend at fucking Equinox. Her very first day at Cambridge, her next-door neighbor took her on a tour of campus, pointed out a weeping willow, and told her, "That's where I kissed this American girl I know. Just not yet." Meanwhile, I was being treated with cruelty or indifference by the men I dated. I didn't know how to make it better, so I made it a joke I told at my own expense to my friends over drinks and even in Caroline's book. She never asked me to, but I used my own assault as a punchline to make her West Village boyfriend seem all the more perfect—*"You're dating Ted Bundy," [Natalie said,] "The apple picking comes right before the strangling. And I should know, as I myself was just sexually strangled in Bay Ridge."*

But the bar in Amsterdam was warm and the wine quickly became complimentary. Caroline had a way of drawing the world into her. The bartender kept sliding drinks our way, and I thought, *Why not try being coy and optimistic for once? Why not try being like Caroline?*

As the bartender counted the till, I told Caroline I was staying behind to have an adventure. "He's so cute!" she whispered, and told me she would take the Airbnb key and get to work on a paper for class. We hugged goodbye, and she pulled on her fur, positioned herself on the back of a stranger's bike, and was whisked away.

"Where'd your friend in the dress go?" the bartender finally said.

I told him she had a boyfriend in the Swedish military, but that I didn't.

He told me his apartment was too far away, but we could go to the bathroom.

The bathroom, I knew, was a single stall in an unfinished basement. There was wet toilet paper on the ground and mold on the walls. I sighed and asked him to take me home.

Ten minutes later, I was deposited outside the apartment Caroline had rented. So I had been sexually rejected by a bartender—not the first time, wouldn't be the last. I buzzed the door, but Caroline didn't answer. I called her cell, which rang, and left Facebook messages that showed up as delivered but unread. It was two in the morning, but one of the worst nights of my life was just beginning. Whether I huddled on the stoop, walked with my head down, or camped out in a train station, men always found me. I was harassed by a group of drunk Irish teenagers, Dutch crust punks, and a DJ who told me he wrote poetry about murdering Natalie Portman. An old man grabbed my hand and kissed it, and a chef with braces found me hiding in a stairwell and tried to take me home with him via ferry. As the sun rose, a Starbucks barista told me I looked terrible and let me wash my face in the industrial sink, and as the city opened, I tried to get some sleep in the bathroom stall at the Fotografiemuseum, but the automatic toilet kept flushing. Throughout the ordeal, I kept attempting to contact Caroline. I became convinced something terrible had happened when we parted ways. Soon I'd have to identify her body, I thought, rehearsing what I'd say to her boyfriend.

But then at noon, she finally answered the door. Yawning, she asked me how my adventure went.

I pushed past her, shedding my filthy clothes in the hallway. "You have no idea what I went through last night," I remember shrieking. "Why didn't you answer your phone?"

She told me she assumed I was home with the bartender.

"This is what I tried to tell you," I said. I stood in front of her in just my leggings and a bra, sobbing stupidly. "Men treat me differently than they treat you. Everyone does." I collapsed into the rented bed. Caroline hovered over me, weeping, too. "And the really messed-up thing is that whole night I thought something terrible had happened to you," I said. "But you forgot I existed."

"I'll never leave you alone with a man again," she said.

"That's not the point, Caroline. I need to know you're on my team!"

As I fell asleep she stroked my hair, and I could hear her saying over and over, "You're so precious to me, you're so precious to me." I believed she meant it, but that didn't matter anymore.

After Amsterdam, I stayed for a couple weeks and kept working but simmered with hurt and rage until I returned to Brooklyn. It was spring—Caroline graduated, I got a day job harvesting lettuce on top of the Gowanus Whole Foods, and I stopped returning her messages. I'd always known she couldn't arrive at the airport at the suggested time, be bothered with classwork, take care of the King Charles spaniels she impulse bought, but I had held on to the fantasy that she didn't care about that small stuff because she was busy with the grand plans that would change my life. I had built my whole career around my commitment to her persona—crafting it, caring for it, and trying my hardest to copy it, spinning out onto the streets of a strange European city as if the world existed to take care of me. But in Cambridge I didn't see someone I wanted to be but a girl living with one fork, no friends, and multiple copies of *Prozac Nation*. Now I saw Caroline for what she was—a person in need of help that I didn't know how to give.

And yet, even after I moved to LA in the fall of 2016, we still had a deadline and kept trying to write the book together, this time via Skype. We'd stare into each other's pixelated faces as I attempted to coax the sentences out of her. Caroline looked like she was in pain as she wrote, gritting her teeth and turning away from the screen like she was reaching through a blizzard to type. The last time we saw each other in person that winter in New York, I was introducing her to the man I'd one day marry; as an early birthday gift, she gave me already-used Glossier makeup and a check that bounced. She offhandedly promised me all the film-TV rights to the book. The book that she still couldn't write. Back in LA, I bought us time with the publishers by writing a quarter of the manuscript by myself, but Caroline hated it so much that she threatened suicide if I wrote anymore. After she said that, I pulled away and watched in real time on Instagram as she counted down the days until she missed the final deadline for her book contract. Caroline claimed her failure to write the manuscript was an intentional stand against the patriarchy and a publishing industry that insisted her life story be defined by the men she dated. Anyway. Her publishers asked her to return over

$100,000. (Caroline says she's continuing to work on a resolution with the publisher.)

We had fights both stupid and serious. "Why does your self-actualization have to come at the expense of people close to you?" is something I said to her. Caroline's response: "It's important to me to make the things I feel are important to make without anyone telling me what to do... If you feel that it's harming you emotionally or professionally, I think you should examine those feelings in yourself." I got work at a pencil store and told her via email that we were through.

Since then, Caroline has become for me something to explain during job interviews, a party anecdote. People ask me if she's a female Billy McFarland, both characters from *Ingrid Goes West*, Anna Delvey with an art-history degree, but I push back. If it was just money and fame she was after, all she had to do was be quiet and let me do the work. She could have been paid hundreds of thousands of dollars, gone on the tour she always wanted, and recorded the audiobook in that beguiling voice of hers. But she had to be the one to tell her own life story, even if she couldn't. Caroline was caught between who she was and who she believed herself to be, which in the end may have been the most relatable thing about her. This is why, when people ask me if Caroline is a scammer, I try to explain that if she is, her first mark is always herself.

Caroline and I hadn't spoken in two years until I reached out to tell her I was publishing this essay. I wrote too many versions of that email, some drafts still furious at her, another calling myself the fox in the henhouse of her life. I still couldn't help apologizing to her even as I tried to explain that after five years of losing myself in our friendship, I needed to be something more than a supporting character in her life. In her response, she told me she loved me, this essay will make her life so much harder, I'm the best writer she knows, she's off Adderall now, trolls will tell her to kill herself, she still wants to be friends. And there I was, once again knocked flat by the force of her praise, her self-mythologizing and raw sentimentality. Part of me longed to keep talking to her, once again warmed by the glow of her attention. Most of all, though, I wanted to ask her what she was still doing on Instagram. When our eyes locked across that workshop table seven years ago, the world felt bigger than a square of light on our phones, and for a while, internet writing was only a means to an end, a way to launch a book that would be as real as we believed our friendship to be. But I suspected if I sent Caroline that email, she would just screenshot it and post it to her feed like she did my first message, turning a moment between us into just another chapter in the story she can't stop telling.

HOW MAY I HELP YOU?

I smelled the smoke snaking through the open door before I saw her. The San Gabriel Mountains were engulfed in flames that day, and though ash floated downwind onto York Boulevard, the shops remained open. The woman wore a linen jumpsuit the color of a matcha latte and would have been indistinguishable from all the other Eastside white ladies if not for her face, which was grim and bloodless, her jaw clenched so tight I wanted to offer a wooden spoon to bite down upon. She picked up a brass pencil sharpener and quizzically turned it around in her hands before setting it down in the wrong place. I made a mental note to move it back when she left.

"Can you help me?" she asked.

"That's what I'm here for," I said. "Are you looking for anything in particular?" I had been a shopgirl, on and off, for eight years, and already knew that this woman was looking for something extremely specific. A notebook for her first day of medical school? Gift for a wayward boyfriend? Of one kind or another, a silver bullet.

"You wouldn't have any 'I'm really sorry' cards?" she asked.

I told her we had sympathy and get well soon.

"I'm looking for something more like, 'sorry I drove my car through your living room,'" she said, trying to laugh it off.

Yup, there it was. Her need filled the one-room store as ripe as body odor.

I kept my face right and instead of asking any car crash follow-up questions, I jogged around the counter and showed her the card shelf featuring illustrations of angels and Band-Aids. Together, we decided the "ugh this sucks" card was too flip, while "thinking of you" seemed unapologetic. "This one feels right!" the woman said, pointing at one that read "I'm sorry" with a drawing of a stick figure facedown on the floor.

"I think you're onto something," I said, considering it. "But doesn't it look like the stick figure was the victim of a hit and run? Could send the wrong message."

The woman dropped the card in mock horror and laughed for real this time.

"We're gonna figure it out," I assured, as I pushed the destroyed living room out of my head, and instead turned myself into her accomplice in making things just a little bit better.

I didn't move to the City of Angels to be a shopgirl. The plan was to become a screenwriter, or really anything fabulous enough to land me at the same dinner party as Ricky Jay. But as I'd soon learn selling sympathy cards, life will go wrong in a thousand different directions, which it did for me, and within a few months of pulling into town I was out of both money and serotonin while the rent, as always, was due.

Shorthand is a stationery store in Highland Park, a mile from my apartment and as far from the ocean as you can be while still in Los Angeles. A couple hours after submitting my résumé I sat down with Joel and Rosanna, the owners of the store and married Seattle transplants (they met each other at a coffee-brewing competition). We walked down the block to the cafe where they filmed *Lady Dynamite*, and even though Joel and Rosanna had only been in town a few years, they exchanged pleasantries with everyone we passed like they were townspeople in the opening number of *Beauty and the Beast*. "We made our first friends when I joined the LA moped community and those guys know *everybody*," explained Joel as he paid for my croissant. Throughout the interview I was relaxed and charming, but the entire time my shopgirl ESP jangled in my head like bells attached to a boutique's front door. In that moment, I knew the job was mine if I wanted it. As I listened to Joel and Rosanna explain how they began their business printing birthday cards in their living room, I resigned myself to once again becoming the girl behind the counter. Years of odd jobs had brought me to a new city with nothing but some silly experiences and a mangled résumé. Since high school, retail had always been my fallback, and here I was, once again falling back. With gratitude and despair, I took the job.

My first day I reminded myself that onboarding at a new store is like stepping in front of the *Honey I Shrunk the Kids* ray gun. A shopgirl inhabits a kingdom in miniature, governed by details as small as a SKU number or a child's fingerprint on a display case. My livelihood depended upon mastering this minutia. On the lacquered plywood display tables and shelves, each notebook, highlighter, stapler, lead refill was color-blocked—picture obedient confetti, Josef Albers but for selling sticky notes, a grid of our signature colors peach and mint, punctuated with shimmers of graphite popping against clean white walls, a layout that looked immaculate in person and, crucially, on Instagram. I felt as though I worked inside a hollowed-out sugar cube, or depending on my mood, an asylum.

A plate glass window separated the retail experience from the letterpress studio in the back. This way, customers could watch the Heidelberg churn out cards without hearing the grind of machinery or smelling the sharp acetone and ink. Cultivating a sense of effortlessness was paramount. For customers, Shorthand should feel like back-to-school shopping—the adolescent giddiness that accompanies a blank notebook and new pack of markers, the confidence that this is finally the semester you'll be organized—only now you're an adult; your graph paper is lavender and you use it for bullet journaling instead of pre-calc. Stepping into the store, I learned, should evoke the same pangs of anticipation and nostalgia as receiving a letter from an old friend. Call me grandiose, but I believe that the ability to facilitate these emotions in a customer is nothing short of what separates a shopgirl from a self-checkout machine.

Joel was the only man at the company, but back in the day was apparently a customer service prodigy at a Seattle Apple Store, and understood the art of shopgirl work better than anyone I had ever met. He guided me through Shopify, fountain pen maintenance, the in-house gift wrapping style. Every day he wore the same stiff designer jeans as a favor to a stylist friend, who needed them broken in for a world-famous pop star. (Joel was always happy to help and also had a great butt, all the shopgirls agreed.) Joel was one of those people who was mysteriously good at everything; photography, house building, motorcycle stuff, and most of all, making people feel at ease. Early on, I greeted customers by leaping off my stool and blurting, "What can I help you find?" until Joel gently corrected my approach. "Our customers don't want to be hustled into making a purchase," he told me. "This isn't New York." (Joel couldn't abide New York as a concept.) "We want them to feel like the store is their living room and we're just happy to chill."

I first became a shopgirl when I was seventeen at Best Video in Hamden, Connecticut. My family had been going there since I was a kid, and you could track my whole childhood through our rental history, from *Balto* to *Bend It Like Beckham* to *Superbad*. The store's higher-ups were two boomers, both named Hank and two others named Richard, plus the beatnik Floatin' Fred and a few other old-timers whose ranks were padded by a platoon of film kids, who knew Tarantino started out at a store just like this one. As the new girl I made the Connecticut minimum wage of eight dollars an hour and pulled the suckiest shifts—Friday to close, Sunday opener—but the free rentals made it worth it. After clocking out I'd collect a stack of DVDs, mostly to prepare for conversations with the college boys of my future—*Reservoir Dogs*, *Oldboy*, and of course *Clerks*, almost required viewing to work there.

"This job would be great if it wasn't for the fucking customers," Randal Graves famously bitches in that movie. At Best Video, I actually loved helping out the fucking customers, and understood that I wasn't hired for my work experience or deep knowledge of the French New Wave, but because I was polite and chatty and when a dad came in looking for movies for his sick daughter, I could merrily lead him around the store, pulling titles while expounding on the cultural importance of Amanda Bynes. When I wasn't with the customers I restocked kettle corn, looked up the rental histories of all my crushes, and dealt with vomit, more of it than I anticipated. Dogs, kids, I think they just got excited. As the rookie I was on puke patrol, and many a shift found me on my hands and knees as I shoveled half-digested kibble into a garbage bag while making small talk with a crowd of disgusted customers. Best Video was my first real job, but from the start it felt like second nature because in a sense it was. Just living as a girl was its own form of vocational training. Everything you'd want the girl behind the counter to be—polite and conciliatory, punctual, clean, meticulous, winsome—had always been expected of me. It became obvious as I greeted customers, dusted the shelves, deflected come-ons, and soothed tantrums, that while Randal Graves and I might have had the same job, he was a clerk, and I was a shopgirl.

You'd be forgiven for assuming that as long as shops have been around, there have been smiling girls stationed within them, girls and retail designed for each other like a spoke and wheel. And yet. Before shopping became a leisure activity in the nineteenth century, stores were staffed by the owner's sons or male apprentices, and when women did retail work it was usually unpaid labor for the family business, an extension of their domestic responsibilities. Even when working, the girls stayed home, and as industrialization increased, cities and by extension, public life, were built to accommodate only men.

This all changed with the advent of department stores such as Marshall Field's in Chicago and Selfridges in London, retail palaces built on the rise of mass production and the wild premise that women wanted to shop. "Get the women and you'll sell the world," opines Octave Mouret, the scion of the department store The Ladies' Paradise, the center of Émile Zola's 1883 novel of the same name. Described by Zola as the "great seducer," Mouret makes his fortune stoking desire in women by turning conspicuous consumption into a religion, one where women are at once acolytes, supplicants, and deities unto themselves. "He was building a temple to Woman, making a legion of shop assistants burn incense before her, creating the rituals of a new cult." Real-life department store magnates like Rowland Hussey Macy and Edward Filene—who described his store as an "Adam-less Eden"—catered to women customers much like Shorthand did, by making them feel at home. In their heyday, department stores provided plush lounge areas, nurseries and children's matinees, personal shoppers, tea shops, and increasingly, a phalanx of pretty young female employees. It was just good business. Women wanted to buy hosiery and cosmetics from other women, and the store owners reasoned that shopgirls were cheaper to hire and less likely to come to work drunk or unionized. Soon, the rise of fixed prices replaced the bartering system, further pacifying the relationship between customer and salesperson. The girl at the counter could now exclusively function as a well-manicured cog in the commercial mechanism.

Off the clock, a new class of citizen poured into the world; as department stores changed the lives of their affluent female customers and newly wage-earning shopgirls, the influx of women changed the cities themselves. With money of their own, throngs of shopgirls moved out of their fathers' houses and filled the dance halls and movie theaters, putting themselves in the company of dateable men. Social etiquette bent to allow women to dine and drink unchaperoned. The practice of window shopping (in French *lèche-vitrines*, or "licking windows") transformed sidewalks from utilitarian pathways to sites where women gathered to take in the latest fashions. Forced to reckon with the influx of women in public and the economic swing from production to consumption, cities installed streetlights and rerouted freight traffic around business centers. Police forces expanded to forcibly remove vice districts, separating prosperous female shoppers from sex workers, the unhoused, or any other unsavory element who threatened the respectable flow of capital.

"Don't panic, but we received a Yelp review," Joel informed my coworker Ellen and me one morning.

For shopgirls, a new Yelp review is like getting your Pap smear results back. At Best Video we got one complaint about customer service and I spent the next two and a half years offering every person who came into the store a glass of water, just in case. At my sister's job at a trendy cookie shop, management would print out and annotate bad Yelp reviews, posting them in the employee lounge like severed heads on spikes.

"We don't know which of you was working when this customer came in, but we should talk about it," Joel continued. "This young lady says she was ignored and made to feel unwelcome, and she says she wasn't helped because she's Mexican."

There was a shame-filled pause between the three of us. I raced through my memory of the previous week, trying to recollect the ethnicities of everyone who had entered the store during my shift. Of course we served Mexican customers. Of course I wouldn't racially profile and ignore someone. Right? But Ellen spoke fluent Spanish and was in school to become a social worker specializing in at-risk youth. No matter how innocent I felt, everyone knew that I was the likely culprit.

When I moved to town, Highland Park was in the grip of gentrification. Customers were quick to tell me how fast the neighborhood had changed. "Ten years ago you couldn't stand on a corner without getting shot," and "I can't believe a stationery store can even exist here." The block itself was a mix. A party supply store that sold Trump piñatas to pulverize, an acai bowl spot, a dusty antique store where you could also renew your vehicle registration. This was the same intersection where, eighteen years ago, Mr. Pink collided with the Chevy's windshield in *Reservoir Dogs*, but is now used as a backdrop for Pepsi commercials starring Gillian Jacobs. There were fliers around the neighborhood that read, "You're the reason my cousin has to commute an hour to school." One night I bit into a taco from the Estrella truck that was so spicy I had to dash into the French bistro next door and gulp down a milk-based cocktail, which even as it was happening felt emblematic. A few years before I arrived, the 2008 recession chummed the water for house flippers, and the median cost of a house in the neighborhood increased from $350,000 in 2010 to $800,000 today. Legacy businesses closed, rents tripled. Students at the high school resorted to sleeping in their cars as their parents were priced out of town. By the time I arrived in 2016, the white population threatened to outnumber the Latinx residents who had made the neighborhood their home since white flight in the 1960s. Every month new businesses opened on York and Figueroa that catered to these new residents, from an upscale bowling alley to a bar offering small-batch IPAs and shuffleboard on the patio, and of course, the very store I worked at.

Then again, Shorthand wasn't Paper Source. Joel and Rosanna did not have VC funding. Our fanciest pencil cost $2.50. How harmful could a vibe possibly be? Maybe I was projecting my own guilt onto a mom-and-pop shop that had almost nothing to be sorry for.

It's impossible to know if I was there the day the writer of the Yelp review came in. What I do know is that since their inception, shopgirls have served as constant gardeners of segregation. Back in the golden age of department stores, a shopgirl's helpfulness was never equal opportunity, but first and foremost about protecting the brand of the store itself. Historically, shopgirls discouraged undesirable customers with intentionally shoddy service or by passive-aggressively directing patrons of color to the bargain basement. None of which is revelatory. We all remember what happened when Oprah tried to buy that handbag in Zurich.

I still wonder, though, if I did more damage to the neighborhood not by badly serving Latinx customers, but rather by providing superlative service to the gentrifying clientele. After all, there I was each day, welcoming a flood of bougie white people into a store that I made to

feel like their living rooms, letting them know that Highland Park was just one more place that belonged to them.

The second time I learned a new POS system was for my
college job at a prop shop in Gowanus, Brooklyn. Film Biz
Recycling gave me ten bucks an hour, a 90 percent employee
discount, and due to a sponsorship with Brooklyn Brewery,
free after-work beers. Founded by a disillusioned production
designer—she had spent tens of thousands of dollars buying and shipping live trees for a commercial shoot, only for
the director to demand at the last minute that the trees get
trashed in exchange for plastics—Film Biz took in donations of used wardrobe, set design, and all the random crap
you need to make a movie that would otherwise be joining
those trees in a dumpster. The shopgirls (and for most of the
time, it was all young women who worked there) would
sort through the material and send it along to shelters and
public school art programs, pulling aside the nice furniture
and industry props to be sold in the store—breakaway glass,
anything Mid-Century Modern, the prop electric chair. We
rented out a real bear skin rug, head intact, and customers would sometimes cut their fingers on its canines. Even
dead, the bear could still draw blood. The place was held
together with gaffer tape and grant money and operated as
a not-for-profit, not that we could have made money if we
wanted to. Above the toilet there was a power switch accompanied by a sign that warned, "Do not flip this switch!
We will literally drown in shit!"

But no one ever did and I stuck around for three years,
to this day the longest I've ever held a job. Sure there were

the usual indignities—Black Friday, a dead mouse rotting somewhere under a donation from *The Dark Knight Rises*—but there was something life-affirming about the job. The simplest explanation is that I got to wear a tool belt. The work required cheerfully ringing out a customer and then muscling their purchase into a taxi or cube truck, a quick change from Retail Barbie to manual laborer that, now that I consider it, probably activated latent gender dysphoria, but at the time felt like eating a meal comprised of all the major food groups. If only it could have lasted, but the good jobs never do. A year after Hurricane Sandy the grants stopped covering overhead, the landlord ramped up his campaign of terror, and the store was stripped for parts and shuttered. It was time for me to find a real job, whatever that meant. Where could I go, other than another store? Over the years I had watched the production assistants screech into the parking lot on their way to soundstages in Astoria, the carrot of a promotion practically dangling off the windshield of their Sprinter vans. Those poor souls had bought into the myth that it was possible to work your way up in the film industry. As a shopgirl, I knew better. There was no upward mobility, only a paycheck and a counter to lean on until your real life started.

That spring, a rich man and his wife came into Shorthand. I hadn't been in town that long, but already I knew these were Pacific Palisades or Santa Monica ocean-breeze-and-a-view types. You just didn't see men wearing loafers in this part of town. The rich man was cruel to his wife but nice to me. They stayed for over an hour. She continually piled merchandise on the counter while he rested his elbows on the glass display case and grilled me on my life outside of Shorthand. He was a producer, of course, with one very famous comedy to his name. He saw a spark in me, he said, and wanted to help my career. When they left I found his name in the Sony hack and learned he was a "profit participant" in a series of syndicated game shows for which he was paid sixty-nine million dollars. Nauseating! But useful? I knew this had been an act for this guy, the role of mysterious benefactor, wish granter, the man you meet by chance and your life is never the same. But also…this was LA, where starlets were once discovered at soda fountains. Why not screenwriters at pencil stores?

In 1948, a twenty-seven-year-old Patricia Highsmith, "feeling vaguely depressed and short of money," took a job as a shopgirl at a Manhattan department store. Though she had finished her first novel *Strangers on a Train*, it would be a year until its release, and so for a while longer she was just another seasonal employee selling baby dolls with real human hair. After filling an order for a radiant blonde woman in a mink coat, Highsmith felt "odd and swimmy in the head, near to fainting yet at the same time uplifted." After work she wrote an eight-page story about the woman, and the next day she almost fainted again, this time on the subway, sick, she'd learn, with chickenpox. "One of the small, grubby-nosed children there must have passed on the germ, but in a way the germ of a book too: fever is stimulating to the imagination," she wrote in the afterword of *The Price of Salt*, the book that the short story would grow into. As a young writer, Highsmith suffered through the Christmas rush, a 104-degree temperature, and months peppered with bleeding spots as if "hit by a volley of air-gun pellets" and emerged on the other side with the story of Therese Belivet and Carol Aird. I hoped there was a lesson here, or better yet, a map. Highsmith's advice? "One must not scratch [pustules] in one's sleep, otherwise scars and pits result," and quit your job after two-and-a-half weeks.

The longer I stayed a shopgirl, the harder it became to pretend that the job wasn't who I was. As an hourly employee, the passage of time had a particularly tight grip on my sense of self. It didn't help that at Shorthand the cash register sat beneath a 3x12-foot Stendig calendar mounted to the wall. Through my shift, the Helvetica days and weeks loomed over me until it was once again time to clamber up the stepladder and tear off another spent month. I tried to wring some glamor out of the position by reporting back to my New York friends that my job was selling pencils to character actors. I'd ring up Britt Lower, Maria Bamford, the tall dweeb from *Legally Blonde* who Elle slaps. ("Sorry for what? For breaking my heart?! Or for giving me the greatest pleasure I have ever known and then just taking it away?!") I'd recognize comedians from Mike Schur sitcoms, clock the names of *This American Life* contributors on their credit cards as they paid for Midori yearly planners. It is easy to slip into self-pity while handling other people's money. I couldn't help it. I had moved to LA to work in the pictures, but here I was, stuck helping Millie from *Freaks and Geeks* choose the right glue stick.

From the jump, I tried not to befriend my pencil shop coworkers. I ignored the group chat. Biked home without meeting anyone for happy hour. Then as the months passed and the gig became my day job and then my life, I reluctantly gave myself over to the social world of the store. Ellen was the most senior shopgirl, who in addition to pursuing her degree in social work, taught wheel throwing at a local pottery studio. Then there was Serena who wanted to be an interior designer and Liv, an actress. Fiona, it turned out, thought she deserved our boss Rosanna's job, and so she didn't last long. In the back were the letterpress girls, Michelle and Tina, who operated the heavy machinery, like the Imperial paper cutter with its twenty-three-inch blade. They were salaried and practiced an actual trade, the kind you took classes for, but even they didn't plan on sticking around forever. Michelle spent her nights doing whatever aspiring improv comedians do and Tina had a degree in college administration and needed to find a way to pay for her three-hundred-person Vietnamese wedding.

As for Joel and Rosanna, they had it all figured out. Just a few years back they had been running the print shop out of their rented house. It's hard to even imagine the floorboards supporting the weight of the iron letterpress. Now they had a storefront, staff, customer loyalty cards. Rosanna handled inventory, card design, and marketing. Joel photographed the products for the website, built the store furniture, and fixed anything that needed fixing. They had a Chihuahua mix named Lucy, threw boozy staff parties at the mini golf course and afterward insisted on stuffing my bike in their trunk and driving me home. I knew that I needed to at all costs avoid the trap of allowing my workplace to become a family, but it was difficult to set that boundary when I was working for an actual family who seemed so happy together. It became even more of a challenge later that year when my sister joined the staff and Rosanna gave birth to a baby girl, who was soon crawling around the workshop as the presses churned away.

Weekend mornings were my favorite shifts, alone with the erasers and cardstock, the smell of carbon black and pencil shavings. Before opening I'd gulp down my fancy cold brew (which cost thirty minutes of work), and tidy the displays while blasting an album I couldn't play during store hours, usually *To Pimp a Butterfly* or the cast recording from the *Buffy* musical episode. At 11:00 a.m. I'd drag out the sandwich board, flip the sign on the door to Open, and the neighborhood would fill the store—school kids knocking their backpacks into towers of notebooks, grandmothers buying Easter cards in bulk, sometimes a kid would come in holding a gerbil and I'd just roll with it. I was good at what I did. Sharpen pencils with three quick twists of the wrist, count change, smile, dust, squeegee, sell. I could rattle off the difference between ballpoints and rollerballs, brush pens, fountains, gels, highlighters. I knew the history of the Blackwing pencil company, how to replace the blades of a double-wedge sharpener, which markers were smudge resistant, quick drying, odor-free. Without realizing it, I became an expert in pushpins and binder clips, A5 envelopes, washi tape, and gift wrapping, although what I knew best of all were the customers.

"Well, what does your nephew like?" I asked the graying hippie in Birkenstocks.

"I'm not sure? Guns?" he guessed. We settled on a field notebook and black ceramic pen, as masculine as you could get at a stationery store.

"It's the thought that counts," I constantly assured customers panicking over a gift.

"What should I get someone who's not my girlfriend but I want her to be?" wondered a middle-aged woman.

"What's an appropriate gift to send after a job interview?"

"What crafting supplies do you recommend for adult anxiety?"

"How late is too late to send a sympathy card?"

Soon I knew more about the inner lives of our regulars than I did about the city I lived in. It wasn't so bad, to spend my day solving problems with attentiveness and cotton ribbon tied in a bow. "Let's see what we can figure out," I'd repeat until close and I was alone again, counting the till in the dark store.

One slow afternoon I was untangling a ball of twine when a man strolled in with his dachshund. He smiled as he approached the counter. "I just want to let you know,"

he said, still grinning, "that you are a slave to money."
He wore pleated linen trousers and huaraches, his man
bun held back with a purple scrunchie. "Money is your
god," he continued. "Can't you see? It's all around you."

When your job is to welcome everyone who walks
through the front doors, it can be hard to know how to
push back on customers, when to let your personal security gate lower over your face. The problem is, creeps
love shopgirls. We're sitting ducks, eye candy, a captive
audience, and the weird men demanding our time were
the biggest clichés of all. At Shorthand we'd get day
drinkers stumbling into the displays and trying to steal
shit, asking me to ditch and get a beer from Johnny's Bar
next door. Then there were your standard lonely hearts,
men who never bought anything but would sketch portraits of the shopgirls on the test pads. Once a guy with
bleeding, chapped lips introduced himself as an "entre-
preneur" and asked if he could borrow the Heidelberg to
make T-shirts for his streetwear line. When I told him
it wasn't for sale and wasn't a screen printer, he leaned
over the counter and shouted that I didn't know what I
was talking about because I wasn't Elon Musk. "Ha-ha,
guilty as charged!" I trilled in my special, de-escalatory
voice. A shopgirl is sometimes a hostage negotiator, the
hostage being the carefully maintained ambiance of the
store, or sometimes herself. Ellen had a particularly clingy
regular, a film guy who'd shuffle in with xeroxed arti-
cles about Busby Berkeley to discuss with her while she
tried to work.

"Is Ellen here? I found this stellar Astaire photo spread

I think she'd flip for," he asked one day, when it was just me at the counter.

"She's out, so sorry," I said without looking up from bar coding. Eye contact only encourages the repeat offenders.

He asked when she worked next.

"Hard to say. Her hours are way down. She might not come back," I said, which was a lie. The man's face crumpled, but perked up with a new idea.

"Hey! Do you like movies?" he asked.

"No," I said.

There was a pause. "You don't like any movies?" he double-checked.

"Never cared for them."

Working at the video store, my main issue was the occasional man who'd ask me to find titles in the Adults Only section behind the duvetyn curtain. I suppose I could have picked up my skirts (gaucho pants) and run to a male coworker, but when customers made this request I took it as a challenge, and I was the kind of seventeen-year-old who had recently ruined a party by swallowing and throwing up a whole tin of spearmints on a dare. The porn section was disorganized and smelled bad because like the single-stall bathroom, it was a place where customers were unsupervised and so it immediately became disgusting. I was never much help finding *American Booty* or whatever they were looking for, but the point wasn't to find the title—just like the creeps at Shorthand, it was to force a girl to give them attention. I wish these men understood that they didn't need to play games, just spend money. We were at work after all, and our job was helping them exchange dollars for things, whether it was a mechanical pencil or a DVD of *Edward Penis Hands*.

To the outside world, a shopgirl is not so much an employee but the outward face of the store. In Zola's novel, the comely staff of The Ladies' Paradise wear uniforms of black silk, and each girl carries a pencil "plunged into her bosom between the two buttonholes of her bodice," as much a part of the store's decoration as the mannequins draped in fox fur, displaying price tags where their heads should have been. In James Baldwin's 1974 novel *If Beale Street Could Talk*, Tish is hired to work the perfume counter at a high-end department store because in the eyes of the management, a Black girl on the floor makes the store seem daring and progressive. At the real-life Biba, a department store that epitomized swinging sixties London fashion, the shopgirls weren't hired to assist customers (any employee who asked "can I help you" was fired on the spot) but rather to evince an aesthetic. In the words of the store's owner Barbara Hulanicki, the ideal Biba customers were "postwar babies who had been deprived of nourishing protein in childhood and grew up into beautiful skinny people," and it was by design that the shopgirls, who included teenage Anna Wintour, also fit this description. In a sense shopgirls are mascots, and to the public become a synecdoche for the store itself. When The Angry Brigade, a militant anti-capitalist group, bombed the seven-story Biba store on May Day 1971, their communiqué claiming credit for the attack first called out the girls who worked there, "All the sales girls in the flash boutiques are made to dress the same and have the same make-up, representing the 1940's... capitalism can only go backwards—they've nowhere to go—they're dead. The future is ours." The Angry Brigade goes on to ask, "Brothers and Sisters, what are your real desires? Sit in the drugstore, look distant, empty, bored, drinking some tasteless coffee? Or perhaps BLOW IT UP OR BURN IT DOWN. The only thing you can do with modern slave-houses—called boutiques—IS WRECK THEM."

The man with the dachshund spent ten minutes trying to drive his point home. "You are a money slave," he repeated, relaxed but resolute. What did he want? Even if I could have dropped the professional smile and argued, I didn't have it in me. No shit, I was a slave to money. Rent, food, just that morning I left for work only to discover that my bike, while still U-locked to the fence, had otherwise been dismantled and was now in pieces. And so I sold alpaca-shaped paper clips, and when men like this guy wanted a moment of my time, I remained pleasant as always, an engaged audience of one.

By the time I hit the year mark I had become Shorthand's most senior front-of-store employee. Ellen had graduated from social work school. A few others came and went. The lifestyle wasn't something you grew into so much as out of; it's shopgirl, not shopwoman. In the circle of life at a mid-century department store, a shopgirl could expect to either burn out or get married. In fact, snagging a husband was considered one of the perks of the job, and as such, shopgirls were considered immoral strumpets, especially when helping wealthy male customers. *The Ladies' Paradise* ends with our provincial shopgirl falling in love with and marrying the owner of the store. "Look what a chance I've got! Why, one of our glove girls married a Pittsburgh—steel maker, or blacksmith or something—the other day worth a million dollars," exclaims Nancy, the gold-digging shopgirl in the O. Henry story "The Trimmed Lamp." As she waits for Mr. Big, Nancy subsists off dry bread, on her face the "faint, soldierly, sweet, grim smile of a preordained man-hunter." Personally I wasn't in the market for a husband, but I had back taxes and was a Los Angeles bike commuter with no health insurance. I needed an exit strategy, so I took a page out of Nancy's book and reached out to the sixty-nine-million-dollar man. A few days later we were on the phone, and he was assuring me he would help out. We spoke for over an hour, him going on about the idea retreats he attends with his cohort, the undeniable spark he saw in me, blah blah blah. Who knows if anything would have come of it, what compromises I might have made, because the very next day the Weinstein story broke, and he never corresponded with me again.

It was just supposed to be a day job, but the day never seemed to end. At Film Biz I remember pitying my older coworkers. *You're already twenty-seven and you still work retail*, I thought at the time. *Can't you see, you're never going to become a cinematographer!* Now I was just like them, only further from the work I wanted to be doing. The early pride I felt in color blocking displays of highlighters had officially curdled. What had brought me to this point, where I found gratification in selling ten dollars' worth of paper clips? How had my life become so inconsequential? Isn't the lesson of stationery that erasers scrub down to nothing, pens run dry? I, too, was spent. My bitterness soon leaked across the entirety of the job, from the repetitive Spotify playlists to rewriting the sidewalk sign after someone changed it from "Great Pens Sold Here" to "Great Penis Here." I lost patience with the Occidental students blowing their allowances and the boomers who, while paying for a stack of greeting cards at a bustling card shop, wanted me to know that "people don't actually send cards anymore."

I was especially sick of the customers who didn't know how to choose a card that would say what they meant, despite the fact that dozens of proclamations of love and sympathy and congratulations had been pre-articulated and cued up on shelves like automatic email replies. Why did all these people need my help? I had already inspected, folded, packaged, dusted, and displayed the cards, and now they wanted me to walk them through the semiotic gradations between "Love You, Boo," "Be Mine," and "All My Favorite Songs Sound Like You"? Their neediness infuriated me. I was done.

A shopgirl becomes useless when she hates the customers for shopping. There must be some of us out there who stay enthused and meticulous forever, who never get bored of the unending onslaught of people asking for things. These lifers deserve some sort of reward; I propose gold-plated scissors for cutting both ribbon and unpleasant customers, which a long-term shopgirl has earned the right to do. As for me, after eight cumulative years behind a counter, it was time to go. Mysteriously, Joel had lost the hearing in his left ear, and as I put in my two weeks I wondered if I would ever find out what was up with that. Scrambling once again, I reformatted my résumé, exaggerated my Shorthand responsibilities to the breaking point, called in favors, and even emailed the sixty-nine-million-dollar man one more time—"If you come across anyone looking for a scrappy assistant or PA or really any other position that isn't intrinsically evil or in retail, I'd be eternally grateful if you thought of me," I wrote, but predictably, received no response. After a few weeks I used a professional contact from my boyfriend to score my first full-time office job, as an assistant at a film company in Beverly Hills. I had at last found work in the industry, and what a relief it was to no longer be just another service worker with a BFA, caught between what I did and who I was.

At my new job, I took meeting notes on Shorthand stationery, but when my boss mentioned that she loved the store, I didn't reveal that the last time she was in I probably served her. I already felt like a child in disguise, dressed up in blouses and computer glasses, trying very hard not to ruin the spreadsheets I was in charge of. The office itself, where I spent fifty hours a week, was operating-room clean, outfitted with glossy white tables and posters for *Exit Through the Gift Shop*, sealed by glass doors that could only be opened with a keycard. At last I was out of the public's reach, but free to do what, exactly? "What I want to do in *The Ladies' Paradise* is write the poem of modern activity," wrote Zola. "Hence, a complete shift in philosophy: no more pessimism, first of all. Don't conclude with the stupidity and sadness of life. Instead, conclude with its continual labor, the power and gaiety that comes from its productivity. In a word, go along with the century, express the century." As an assistant, my continual labor was mostly spent on email, "just circling back." I sat at my desk and scrolled or Slacked, distant, empty, bored, drinking some tasteless seltzer. Occasionally a screenplay or documentary would land on my desk and slap me to attention, but mostly the job was administrative, and as the months ground on, I felt my posture, once as upright as a LEGO businesswoman's, begin to curl over my keyboard.

When I did the math, I realized that my office salary was basically the same hourly rate I got as a shopgirl, the only difference was that as an assistant there were more hours to fill, often unpaid. In *The Price of Salt*, it's only on her day off that Therese visits Carol's home and drinks a glass of hot milk that tastes of "bone and blood, of warm flesh, saltless as chalk yet alive as a growing embryo." I'm sorry, but you can't write a sentence like that while tied to email. My mistake was believing I could solve my work problems with more work, when what I actually wanted was, you know, to live.

Seven months after I left Shorthand, I learned that Joel had died from complications from brain surgery. The night before the funeral the store filled with body heat from the mourners crowding inside. Rosanna kept the doors open late for the friends and family who had traveled in, and because I didn't know what else to do, I picked up one final shift. We were all there that night, the printmakers, the shopgirls who currently worked there, and those of us who had gone on to other jobs, a group of young women lending a hand. We mostly sold sympathy cards that night, cards designed and printed in the shop Joel co-owned, bought by his mourners, and which would be given right back to Rosanna. At my station behind the counter, muscle memory propelled me through the shift. The work is hard to forget, even if you try. It was the last time I'd ever be a shopgirl.

Back when I gave my two weeks, it seemed that working at Shorthand made my life as small as our smallest product. And it became overwhelming, to feel so trivial and then be faced with the bigness of our customers' needs. Joel was gone. How could a five-dollar card solve this problem? The answer to that, as always, is above my pay grade. But if you had been there that night, in the room that Joel and Rosanna built together, you would have understood what it means to quietly ask a stranger, "How can I help you?" and then actually be able to do it.

ABORTION
ABORTION
ABORTION

The women's clinic is twenty minutes outside the city, and when you walk from your parking spot you're met by the smells of overwatered lawns, frying bacon, truck exhaust, and then all at once, the sweat and church perfume of a dozen Evangelicals accusing you of infanticide. They clog the sidewalk like a chorus line out of step with reality. It feels like you stumbled upon a hateful community theater production—the scenery chewing and AV equipment and props, the banners featuring badly photoshopped fetuses. Who are these people? The answer is both irrelevant and the reason you're out here on this bright Sunday morning, applying sunscreen and summoning courage. You slink through their barricade and feel extremely female, fragile as an Olsen twin in a paparazzi photo, gripping your iced coffee and cowering behind your biggest sunglasses.

At the clinic's side entrance you find your supervisor, a woman with purple hair and no last name. She tosses you a neon vest that reads "Clinic Escort" and "Escolta de la Clinica." It's the kind of garment you'd wear while hiking so a hunter won't shoot you. You think, *Out here I'm the target*, and then get embarrassed by your histrionics. You find out where you're needed. You take your place on the line.

In a previous life (like eleven weeks ago) you were of the mind that life was pretty good and only getting better, and sure there were storm clouds gathering but they were way off in the distance. Then you realized you had been viewing the world through the wrong end of the binoculars.

So you feel like shit. Your leaders have been stripped of power. Your enemies have mobilized. You look for hope in all the wrong places, like Twitter.

Online, everyone is screaming. Your phone becomes the window from which you witness a thousand interlocking catastrophes: emaciated polar bears and caged children and millionaires celebrating the end of healthcare, GoFundMe cancer campaigns and Patreons for unemployed journalists and shaky videos of police murder and arguing, just so much arguing, which is productive you think, but also maybe killing you. Beneath it all, the constant thrum: *no one is coming to save us* and *for the love of god somebody do something.*

So you spend mornings calling your representatives, shrieking into the phone, "Why aren't you trying harder?!" At night you barricade yourself in your apartment and watch all the *Buffy* episodes about depression. And when you do sleep, in clammy fits, you dream of moving stones. The stones are round and weathered and cool to the touch, just heavy enough that you need two hands to carry them from one pile to another. In the dream it's understood that this is your sole responsibility. Not podcasts or petitions or any thinking or talking at all. Your assignment in the group project to save the world. Just move the stones.

At the start of your clinic shift you're stationed in the back lot. It's your job to accompany the client and her companion (that's what you're taught to call them) from their cars to the clinic door. There are more ways than you'd expect to screw up something so simple. Despite the vest, you'll be mistaken as part of the group of "antis" blocking the sidewalk. (The terminology is tedious but important, because we live in a world where the movement that assassinates doctors still gets to call itself "pro-life.") You will learn that even your most innocuous small talk can go wrong; "How are you?" is a loaded question. "Good morning" comes off as presumptuous. Safe areas: weather, football, loungewear. The one thing we can all bond over, you'll learn, is the bedraggled clownishness of the antis themselves, who never stop embarrassing themselves. It's a universal language, dunking on bigots, and the clients love to get in on it.

"Tube sock motherfuckers."

"Fake Christians."

"Bunch of virgins."

You watch as a teenage girl rolls down the window of her white PT Cruiser and exhales a plume of fruit-scented smoke into the face of the man telling her that whores go to hell.

Your favorite, the old woman who couldn't stop giggling as she shouted at the protestors, "Find something else to do!" She accepted a high five from her grand-daughter as they passed through the doors.

With ninety minutes to go you're moved to the front lines. You square your shoulders in a performance of bravery. You bring your toes up to where the asphalt of the clinic's parking lot meets the cement sidewalk. In and of itself, the line is nothing more than a millimeter of air between different types of pavement, but property rights being stronger than women's rights, the antis are legally prohibited from crossing into the parking lot. Your body is there so they don't try to anyway.

You are recognized immediately as fresh meat. The antis' attention swings toward you like the Eye of Sauron in cargo shorts. Your haircut: lesbo. Your soul: doomed. They demand to know how much blood money you're getting paid. They tell you there are plenty of other jobs you could have, for instance, lounge singer(!). And in response, you don't say a goddamn thing. In your training session in the meeting room at the library, you were told it's not your job to listen, persuade, rebut, reason with, or reach across the aisle. The opposite, in fact. You plac-idly absorb their sound and fury like foam stapled to the wall of a garage recording studio.

Later, your friends say they wouldn't be able to silently take that abuse, pull off the whole guard-at-Buckingham-Palace thing. But it's been so long, maybe never in fact, that your body was a tool for good. So you keep going back, and you hold the line.

One night as you're going to bed you hear screams and shattering glass from the apartment unit below you. You hear a woman shouting, "Don't touch me!" You step onto the landing and one story down you see your neighbor Lauren running to the parking lot. A door slams and then her fiancé is running after her. You lean over the metal railing and call to her and she dashes up the stairs and into your living room. You remember your training and fill the doorway and shut the door in the fiancé's face. He fumes outside until Lauren gets a push notification that he's taken a Lyft to a bar. "I've never loved anyone more than him," she tells you. "My parents have already paid for the wedding." She has a tattoo of half an avocado on her forearm, and you hope that the other half belongs to someone who can talk some sense into her. You exchange numbers. She takes him back. From then on, when you run into the fiancé at the trash cans, you give him the look that says, "I know you, ass-hole." When you hear screaming and crying through the floorboards you text to check in. Eventually Lauren responds, "Adults have disagreements. We will keep the noise down. My relationship with my husband is none of your business."

Your fellow escorts are mostly queer ladies who compost and adopt-don't-shop, at least judging from the stickers on their travel coffee mugs. You've committed to small talk so nondescript it evades short-term memory. This is how it has to be. No last names, no jobs, no alma maters, for the same reason some abortion providers go to work wearing rubber Halloween masks. Given the chance, the antis will figure out who you are. From there, addresses, phone numbers, names of family. Throughout the shift they film you, probably for their ghoulish YouTube channel, but also to search for identifying clues. They've long known the names of your supervisors, whose social media posts they'll read aloud and mock.

That's another rule: no posting. It feels good, right? To be forbidden from taking a social justice selfie. To just be in the moment, unphotogenic and banal.

Just as the antis start to recognize you by your haircut, which they're deeply offended by, you come to know them as well. The women arrive in their Sunday service clothes, patent leather kitten heels and tight sweaters the color of Hawaiian Punch. And Jesus Christ, these bitches. Through the megaphone they tell women they're mutilating their wombs, will die of breast cancer, that it's God's will they bear children. "Edify the body of Christ!" they shout at teenage pedestrians just trying to buy a donut next door. Sometimes a client will whirl around and plead, "I wanted this baby!" You watch as a mother and father walk into the clinic, each gripping their small son's hand and singing "Twinkle Twinkle Little Star" to drown out the crowd, which only becomes louder in the presence of a child. On the rare occasions their AV equipment is working, the antis will broadcast the sound of infants crying and crying. Apparently there also used to be Catholics praying the rosary, but the Evangelicals kicked them off their turf. "It was hilarious," your supervisor tells you.

Online, it's become a common refrain that there are *no adults in the room*. The real problem, you think, is that the room is full of adults, and the adults are craven dunderheads.

Some mornings the antis bring their own kids. There's a young Black girl always dressed in pink sequins. She'd prefer to sit in the shade with her chapter book, but a few times each hour her mom will stick a microphone in her hand and make her sing hymns, her voice rising above the traffic. (Is this meant to rattle you? You're thrilled for the musical interlude.) The smaller kids play wild games of tag in their clip-on ties, wrestling inches from the six-lane boulevard. In the early months, you daydreamed about rushing into traffic to shield the children from an oncoming lowrider, proving to the antis that you are not Team Child Death. Over time, this fantasy fades. Maybe it's possible to convert these people, but you're not the one who is going to do it.

Indiana: 1978. The history of abortion clinic defense traces its lineage to the Fort Wayne Women's Health Organization, where a small but dedicated feminist chapter— ok, let's be real, you don't have time for historical context! The work before you is immediate and blunt. A patient walks up to the clinic, the antis lunge toward her. You step between them. She reaches the door and you prepare to do it all over again.

Brick by brick, you build yourself into a wall. When you do speak to the antis, it's to issue a demand. They bum-rush a woman arriving on foot and you say "let her pass" in a voice you don't recognize as your own. You learn that courage is a muscle. But more important than courage is commitment, the ability to make a recurring appointment in your calendar and stick to it. A good day is when nothing happens. It's simple, mindless as bench-pressing. Hold the line, help where you're needed. If the answer to life exists, you think you might find it on the loop from the parking lot to the clinic doors and back again.

The only antis who make you nervous are a pair of squirrelly white dudes. They carry signs from a special street preacher outlet store, and match their outfits—camo and the kind of sunglasses pro golfers wore in the '90s. You're not sure if they're militia members or just dress like they are. Either way, costuming is an early step in the journey toward fascism. Pepper spray and knives weigh down their belts, and Mitch, the leader of the two, wears a big political button that just reads Homo with a red X through it. Mitch has a real failed-preacher energy. For all his enthusiasm, his proselytizing never finds the flow.

"Social Justice is idiots!"

"Pagan stupidity alert!"

"Hitler didn't kill his own people! You people are worse than Hitler!"

"You guys are racist against babies!"

"Someone put LSD on your cereal! You're not hip enough to be a hippie! Fake news, fake life!"

"How dare you ignore God? God will ignore *you*! Trap door, lick of fire, AHHH! That's eternity! Ask a fourth grader. That's fair."

These are all direct quotes. You carefully write them down in your Notes app to savor the asinine transcendence. "An abortion of the mind, this purity," wrote William Carlos Williams.

Anytime a client who looks remotely Latinx arrives, Mitch launches into flailing Spanglish—"No la familia? Muy loco. Living la vida loca!"—eventually devolving into grade school vocab—"Cumpleaños! Escuela! Mamasita!" And when the words really fail him, Mitch marches up and down the sidewalk, jaw slack, moaning "Duhhhhhh duh duhhhhh," his impression, you suppose, of your stupidity.

As clownish as Mitch is, he speaks better with his actions, and in this sense, his message comes through loud and clear. As anti-choice leader Barbara Beavers so succinctly put it, "Mothers should die for their babies, not the other way around."

When you first volunteered you were one in a massive influx of new recruits. In the three intervening years, your fellow escorts have fallen off, left town, needed to take weekend work. On one shift you're stationed alongside a rich lady (the Hermès tote gave it away) who you'd never seen before. Another presidential election is barreling toward you, and she reveals that in the upcoming primary she's excited to vote for a certain small-town mayor, a candidate you distrust, who you could argue lacks the political will to meaningfully protect abortion seekers, and anyone who doesn't recognize that is either gullible or complicit. But then you tally the escorts who showed up that day. You realize if the group was down just one more person, the shift would be canceled. This woman's vote doesn't have the power to swing the election, but her presence on the line makes the difference that day. Incrementally, you learn to extend potential allies the benefit of the doubt, a tactic that in a certain light, could be grace. As the critic Michele Wallace wrote, "For a feminist these days, the trick to feeling coherent is to quickly determine what is irrelevant so that you can ignore it and to keep a strategically flexible concept of what really matters." It helps that at the clinic, what really matters is obvious.

Later that day, two cars peel in bumper to bumper. The first car skids to a stop and two women scramble out and jog toward the clinic. A man exits the second car and chases after them, yelling. The women don't turn around as you usher them inside and close the door. You link arms with your partner, the wealthy woman, as the man tries to force his way past you. When that doesn't work he resorts to screaming through the door how serious he is, that it's *his child you bitch*. He returns to his car and waits with the door open and the motor running. Your supervisor walks over and tells him that the clinic staff have called the police and he should go before they arrive, that the police belong to the same nutty church as the antis do, and he's not safe. He insists on staying. He's crying now. Two squad cars lurch into the lot and the police confront him. As you're taught, you film the encounter. Finally, the man leaves, wiping his eyes. You hope desperately that he never gets the woman alone.

And you just keep at it. You greet women, compliment their pajamas, mock your oppressors. Maybe you take time off to visit your parents, or spend a few months canvassing for a congresswoman who'll get harassed out of office eleven months into her term. Meanwhile, friends of yours have gone down their own paths to radicalization—the anti-car movement, prison abolition, the Extinction Rebellion. Other friends are the same as always. This strikes you as willful, like swimming in one place in a rushing river. It's a common question: Can people change? *Yes, of course, constantly*, you think. Each day the world devours and digests us all, and when we're spit out we're different.

You receive a text from Lauren. She asks if it was true that several years ago she spent the night in your apartment to escape her fiancé. You haven't spoken in ages, not since she told you to mind your own business. Since then you've moved to a different part of town, but heard she had a baby. "We're in couples therapy, and he's saying that I'm making it all up. He's saying I was the one who was violent," she texts you. "But I thought I remembered running into your place. That happened, right?" Yes! Of course it happened! Lauren, he's a liar! You send her a blue block of unpunctuated text, listing off the fights and the crying you heard through the floor, how that night after putting Lauren to sleep in your bed, you sat on the couch in the dark and listened to the man return from the bar and stagger up the stairs to your apartment, rattling the door.

In this line of work, the failures stack up until your knees buckle. And so next time around, when Roe falls and we lose the legal right to an abortion, you will be prepared for the bad news, little good that will do.

Again, you will feel like shit. A while ago you thought courage was a muscle and you had made yourself strong, but thanks to six unelected psychos you'll slide right back to thinking of yourself less as a person than a fragile assemblage of organs. You will grow sick of carrying stones, tired of the whole Sisyphean rigmarole. Where is the peace in constant struggle?

No wonder the antis love to go on about the end of days—praise God, a stopping point! In the Evangelical worldview, on the Day of Reckoning the sinful and unbelieving (that's you!) are tossed into the lake of fire, while eternal life awaits the true believers and aborted fetuses, who get a special exemption. That's because to the anti-choicers, no human is more perfect than the one that doesn't exist. They worship helplessness and innocence as it's a danger to their project to be otherwise. In your darker moments the horror of this will bowl you over: these people are *ascendant*. Mitch is *winning*. Maybe he's already won.

But listen. I've been down this road before, and believe me: nothing is over. In fact, pull yourself together because you'll be holding this line for the rest of your life. Would it help to think of the work not as a choice but a conscription? It's just a thing you do, dealing with these assholes. To them, the very fact of your body makes you impure, fallen. They're smart to fear you. Just look what this body of yours can do. Walking women to their appointments isn't so unlike carrying stones. See? You're already strong enough. You are not helpless, or innocent. You are the opposite of unborn.

THE GOWANUS
DOLPHIN

My first apartment had a name: the Leaning

Brownstone. The moniker was printed on a vinyl awning above the front door, our landlord's way of spinning the fact that the building had sunk sideways into the Gowanus mud, jutting over the sidewalk like a crooked baby tooth. (The *New York Times* even wrote about it under the headline "What's Red and Brick and Not Quite Upright?" The article noted that while the building definitely leaned, it wasn't a brownstone.) My roommates and I moved in the August before our sophomore year of college, emptying the U-Haul with the help of three sets of parents and an insistently helpful man named Waleed who worked at the auto shop downstairs. That night we toasted the end of RAs, keycards, and twin beds. The Leaning Brownstone was not the Chelsea Hotel, not yet anyway. But the three of us had secured a first apartment that was idiosyncratic and borderline squalid, which we understood was a crucial step in becoming real artists. The photos of that night show sparkling Yellow Tail slanting in our plastic flutes.

Technically, my first apartment was on Whitney Avenue in New Haven, Connecticut. My family lived there when I was in preschool and kindergarten, and I remember the bunk bed I shared with my sister and the piano keyboard we found in the building's dumpster that burst into flames when I tried to play it. There was a grass courtyard where we'd play with our fluffy orange cat, his collar tied to a long piece of hot-pink rope. But when we say *first apartment*, we're not talking about a family home. Your first apartment is a space beyond the purview of adult supervision. It's an origin story: Chapter One: Your First Apartment, the moral of which is always: *you have to start somewhere.*

I felt queasy my first week in the Leaning Brownstone. Equilibrium was elusive. In the mornings I'd wake up hanging off the back of my bed, and tumble downhill to the bathroom. My rolling desk chair was a nonstarter. The antique bed frame I'd brought from my parents' basement simply wouldn't hold together at that angle. My roommates and I occupied a three-bedroom on the second floor; it was a railroad unit, maybe fifteen feet at its widest. A previous tenant had written "your beautiful" in pink cursive on the bathroom mirror. The kitchen was so small that we had to choose between a full-size refrigerator and the ability to open the front door. Our solution was to stack two mini fridges on top of one another, and secure them to the wall with bungee cords. "Just don't become a cautionary tale," my mom pleaded. "The college kids crushed by a falling tower of refrigerators."

Michael had found the place. He was good at real estate and the most adult of the group. Maybe I was just dazzled by his sweater collection. We had met in writing class our freshman year, and I wanted so badly to impress him that I lied about having seen the Laura Linney movie *The Savages* and then took him to a head shop on Sullivan Street to buy fake IDs. We spent the rest of the semester pretending to be twenty-two-year-olds from Gary, Indiana, and getting drunk off electric lemonade Four Loko, lying on his dorm room carpet listening to the Mountain Goats. As a joke, we'd impersonate a bad one-act play; Michael would shout, "You don't understand me!" and I'd scream back, "*You're* the one who doesn't understand *me*!" After we moved into the Leaning Brownstone, Michael tried to assemble his new IKEA bureau using screws he picked up from the hardware store. When the drawers wouldn't close, his eyes went black. I watched as he ripped the thing apart with his hands, dragged the pieces down the stairs, and dumped them on the curb. That night I realized that Michael didn't have access to a secret cache of adult wisdom, no matter what I'd projected onto him. Feeling overwhelmed, I closed the door to my room and cried. (Still, though, my very own room to cry in! It wasn't lost on me.)

When classes started we all commuted together like siblings walking to the school bus stop. This is also when the apartment started falling apart. A pipe burst and scalding water gushed downhill into the bathroom. I flung open the kitchen cabinet and for the first time in twenty years on this planet, I asked myself how a sink worked. The following week the pilot light went out and when the smell of gas filled the apartment, we thought we were all going to die. (Our landlord was useless, but the ConEd operator clearly had experience with first-timers.) Our upstairs neighbor started to blast what I couldn't describe as music, more like audio of car wrecks layered over static. The noise filled our rooms. When Michael knocked on his door and asked him to turn it down, the neighbor, a wiry bald guy in his seventies, cryptically replied that actually the *worst* thing he could do was turn the music down, otherwise the autistic boy would find him. (I don't feel the need to print the exact word he used—you get the gist.) Hey, at least we didn't have bedbugs.

Our third roommate, Kiran, was a playwright and poet, and had grown up in Sedona, a city so committed to its Southwest woo-woo brand that even the McDonald arches are turquoise. Kiran and Michael had been roommates freshman year, and I once walked in on Kiran with a syringe stuck in his thigh. For months I had agonized over whether I should say something to him about his intravenous drug use, but the joke was on me, it was just testosterone. When we threw our first party at the Leaning Brownstone, Kiran used an extra syringe to inject Capri Sun packets with rum. (I don't think our guests understood what they were drinking because everyone got sick that night. I opened my bedroom door to see a classmate puking out the window.) Over our years of friendship, Kiran would introduce me to burlesque, fat liberation politics, cigarettes (briefly), abolition, and thigh tattoos. We enabled each other's soul food take-out habits, he taught me how to cook with seasoning other than salt and pepper, and he wrote one of my favorite ever plays, about a world where everyone wakes up one day without genitals and needs to figure out new ways to have sex.

Two-thirds of the apartment fucked. Boyfriends were always coming and going—mostly coming, from what I could hear. The wall that separated my room from Michael's was purely ornamental. Lamp light leaked through where the drywall met the floor and ceiling, and we could carry on full conversations at normal volume from our beds. Michael heard me doing push-ups over a can of beans. I heard him deflower Paul. Whenever Michael had a boy over, I'd try to step out on the fire escape or hum loudly, usually "Elbow Room," the *Schoolhouse Rock!* song about manifest destiny that I performed in my eighth grade musical. You boys have fun.

Kiran and I shared an aesthetic and decorating budget, which is to say, we had no money and were happy furnishing the apartment with street finds and actual pieces of garbage, so long as the garbage had personality. In the living room we dragged in a floral grandma couch-bed and the world's ugliest orange-and-green rug, which I considered bohemian. We found a red metal footlocker on the curb, and I helped Kiran make a bed platform out of stacks of wood pallets the NYPD left behind after the marathon. I'd go for walks along the Gowanus Canal and collect pieces of scrap metal, which I'd then hang from fishing line down the wall. On my bedroom door I glued a picture of Christopher Walken's head that I cut from a free *Kill the Irishman* poster. I also glued a wine rack to the wall, frustrated that I couldn't drill through the cement. (The wine rack was the first of many of my projects that crashed to the ground.) Our pride and joy was an IKEA piece of all things, a pinewood table (no particle board here!) called the Norden. It had two wings that could both fold up and down, and six deep drawers. With visions of future dinner parties, we put the Norden in the center of the living room (leveled with a 2x4), right under the inside of a piano I had found in front of the Brooklyn Lyceum, which now swayed from chains screwed into the molding.

In retrospect, Kiran and I were making the apartment uninhabitable for Michael. He wanted to shop at Crate & Barrel instead of the curb, which was more than fair, but also untenable. To make matters worse for Michael, winter arrived and so did the mice. We'd wake each morning to find a small, neat pile of debris and broken glass on the kitchen floor, which for some reason the mice had collected from underneath the oven. From my bedroom I'd hear Michael's tense phone conversations with the super, but to me, the mice were great news, the only excuse I needed to adopt a six-toed tabby cat from a basement in Queens. As a peace offering, I let the boys name her, and being playwrights, they chose Samantha Shepard. Samantha was the light of my life and a grade A asshole. You know, a cat. She'd get herself wedged inside my closet and yowl until I deadlifted the bureau to free her. After using the litter box, she'd emphatically kick her turds onto the bathroom floor. She never caught a mouse, but would use her big mitten-like paws to swat the turkey sandwiches right out of my hands. Michael hated Samantha to such a degree that he needed to put an ocean between them, and announced he was spending the next semester in Berlin. It was a foregone conclusion that when he returned to New York, it wouldn't be to Gowanus. In time, I'd come to learn that to most people, the Leaning Brownstone was cursed. Its aura activated a fight-or-flight response, and Michael was high-tailing it out of there. As for me, it felt like my first real home in the city, which by some definitions, made me a New Yorker. I had found my sea legs.

By my best count, Kiran and I would see sixteen more subletters pass through. After Michael left, our friend Margot took his place, and we spent the whole semester on the couch drinking screwdrivers and screaming about abortion rights. We lived off popcorn, made in the air popper, that Margot drenched in Bragg Liquid Aminos. On Saturdays we'd make a meal we called "two girls, one bowl of pasta." (We both got mono.)

After Margot was Dante. His entire extended family moved him in, but after that he kept to himself. He always wore shower shoes in the bathroom, which made me wonder just how filthy the place looked to everyone else. Later I found a YouTube video featuring Dante rapping about his love for Cornell, which I just couldn't wrap my mind around. My allegiance wasn't to NYU, but the city itself, and I worked hard to maintain the illusion that I was a Brooklynite who just so happened to be taking some college classes.

After Hurricane Irene we fostered a black kitten named Sweet Baby Gene, and being a desert boy, Kiran adopted a tarantula named Pilar. We got a new roommate, an internet writer who, from what I could gather from the phone calls I heard through the walls, was going through an amorphous personal shitstorm. They were on some sort of raw vegan diet, and brought in their own mini refrigerator (the apartment's third, for those keeping track), to store their special macrobiotic food. When the extra appliance made the utilities bill higher than expected, they refused to pay, and the three of us had a vicious argument that came down to whether or not a G Chat exchange constituted a roommate contract. The *E* button on my BlackBerry was busted, so when I kicked them out via text, I wrote, if you'r€ not out now you b€tt€r b€ wh€n I g€t hom€...

We hit the year mark and re-signed the lease. I read Patti Smith's memoir and, trying to capture some downtown romance for myself, took a hammer to our living room wall to expose the brick. (I aborted the mission, and we shifted the grandma couch a foot to the left to hide the hole.) The apartment became a staging ground for our artistic endeavors. Margot swung by to take nude portraits of Kiran. Kiran wrote experimental poetry on the fire escape. When the second season of *Girls* was filming up the block, I ditched my job at the NYU call center to glimpse Lena Dunham watching takes behind the monitor. After we found an espresso machine on the curb on Sterling Place, Kiran would brew me evening cappuccinos and I'd stay up all night writing my magnum opus, a play about a SeaWorld trainer who gets swallowed by a killer whale and spends the rest of the show monologuing from its stomach. The next morning I'd get back up with a couple espressos and print out my scenes on pink paper, which I got free from work and thought would make me memorable and enigmatic in class. That semester, I tried to shoot an avant-garde short film in the bathroom. Kiran operated the camera as I shaved my armpits, footage I then scored to the sounds of a knife scraping burnt toast. Of course after I recorded the audio, I ate the toast. Those days, I was always ravenous.

After a semester studying abroad (and teaching myself to silently masturbate in a room I shared with two other girls), I arrived back at the Leaning Brownstone to discover that our trio of subletters had taken it upon themselves to dismantle the shelving units, remove the wall art, and throw away the rug. Maybe Kiran and I should have asked for a security deposit, but what were we, landlords? That summer Kiran visited his boyfriend's family (they ran an old folks' home in Alaska), and rented his room to Kerry, one of my best friends from home.

Kerry and I had grown up playing soccer together, and as a track star in high school, she was at one time the fastest white girl in Connecticut. I took immense pride in my high tolerance for chaos, but this string of renters had worn me thin. It was a relief to sink into the grandma couch and smoke a bowl with a known quantity.

But the day after Kerry moved in, we heard coughing from the third bedroom. This was a room we had assumed was empty. Kerry and I stood frozen in the kitchen, having a full silent conversation in panicked expressions. *Did someone break in? Should we run? Let's call the cops! Oh, don't be naive! I don't know how to use my mace keychain. What does he want?*

Eventually I called out, "Ummm, who's there?" The bedroom door opened, and out stepped our new roommate, Cavier.

Cavier was a beautiful man. He had rich brown eyes and sharp cheekbones, combined with the insouciance of a minor deity. In my memory, he was shirtless when we met, although that can't be right. It's just from then on, I rarely saw him fully clothed. Anyway, he sat on the couch between me and Kerry and told us he had spent the last several years traveling the world as a model, but quit that "filthy industry" to become an artist. He showed us his work, oversized expressionist faces painted in primary colors on hunks of scrap wood. Sure, I was stoned, but his paintings were remarkable—vivid and emotional and surreal, and I wanted to tell him they reminded me of Basquiat but would that come off as racist? Cavier told us that the room's previous subletter had taken it upon himself to find a replacement, and Cavier had moved in that day when Kerry and I were at work. He called us his "white angels." I passed him my lighter and bowl and he immediately dropped them, scattering embers and shattered glass across the floor.

At first, we were all big fans of Cavier. It didn't seem like an accident that he had appeared in the Leaning Brownstone. He intrinsically got the place. He could roll with it. He didn't care about the apartment's slant or expect me to solve the problem of our neighbor's static broadcasts. Cavier played beer pong with my younger sister when she came to visit and sent his rent directly to the landlord. To prepare for our upcoming soccer seasons, Kerry and I ran wind-sprints at the middle school off 4th, and when we came home Cavier would be brush in hand, painting his masterpiece while shirtless. It was a magical summer. Then Kerry went back to Wesleyan and Kiran returned for the school year. It was an easy choice to make. We all decided that Cavier should sign the lease and make it official.

Right away Cavier brought home a cookies and cream bunny he named Picasso. The bunny was the latest resident in an apartment that now included three people, a tarantula, and a six-toed cat. This didn't count Kiran's boyfriend, Sweet Baby Gene, and the various Mrs. Caviers, who'd walk out of his room in the mornings wearing only stilettos and one of Cavier's paint-stained shirts. Kiran was part of a trans housing network, so occasionally a few girls would crash on the pull-out. Cavier's friend Liam also came through, but when he missed his flight back to Dublin he stayed a whole month. He spent most days on the couch, wrapped in a shawl and strumming his guitar with Samantha on his lap. As a kid in Nigeria, he saw a man burned to death for stealing he told me, although I thought we were just making small talk.

I was alone in the place one evening when a man in a three-piece suit knocked on the door. "Does the artist known as Cavier live here?" he wanted to know. He had seen Cavier selling his paintings in the Broadway-Lafayette subway station, recognized talent, and had come to make a purchase. I was wearing pajamas and was halfway through a bowl of buttered noodles. The man took in the apartment without stepping over the threshold. He told me that as a patron of the arts and as a Black man, he felt a responsibility to collect Black works. He had been on the scene for decades, he said, back when New York was real. "New York feels real to me," I said. He groaned. "You don't actually think that."

When Cavier came into our life, so did the dolphin. He, too, had appeared in Gowanus overnight, swimming in from the harbor. For a few hours he was something of a Gowanus mascot. We all rushed over to the canal to catch a glimpse of his dorsal fin gliding through the oily water. The Gowanus Canal was famed as one of the most polluted waterways in the country. The area was once a creek and wetland, but during industrialization the city razed the landscape to create a transport lane for coal and construction materials, and unintentionally, a depository of raw sewage anytime it rained. To this day, the water contains horrific levels of carcinogens, pesticides, human shit, and more dead bodies than you'd expect so close to a Whole Foods. (It's rumored to be a Mafia dumping ground.) What makes cleaning up so hard isn't the water itself, but the ten-foot layer of industrial sediment on the canal floor. The EPA calls this substance "black mayonnaise." Naturally, we named the dolphin Mucky.

Not that I would have admitted it, but by my third year as a resident of the Leaning Brownstone I began to feel the walls closing in. I was desperately trying to finish my senior thesis, and found the apartment no longer a source of inspiration but anxiety. Meanwhile, I came home from a soccer tournament to discover that Cavier had thrown a party and now all our lights had red bulbs in them. He washed the dishes with Pine-Sol, couldn't tell you why. Pieces of the decor started to disappear— a vintage box of floppy discs I used as a bookend, the sunburst headboard behind the couch, our beloved Norden table—and we realized Cavier was taking things for his art. Then one day I saw Cavier crawling around his room with a hammer, trying to smash whatever was skittering across the floor. At long last, the bugs had breached the walls, stowed away on the pieces of wood Cavier painted. We hung fly paper from every doorway, and when I wasn't paying attention I'd get the sticky pieces stuck in my hair. That fall after a long morning of classes, I returned home to four sets of Eastern European mothers and their teenage daughters sitting patiently in the living room. Despite that one sale, apparently Cavier's painting wasn't covering expenses, so he was taking headshots for aspiring models. God, these poor girls. Trying to make a go of it and instead of a studio, they find themselves with me in the Leaning Brownstone. Wordlessly, I walked through what was now a waiting room and straight into bed, where I buried myself under the comforter and hyperventilated. I was losing my cool, my precious cool! My writing no longer felt like art but homework. My room was filled with empty Red Bull cans because a teammate had gotten a job as a Red Bull Girl, passing out freebies on campus. About to graduate with no prospects for work, I now wondered if I could clean up good enough to join her. (I could not!) Cavier had become the bane of my existence, but more than the bugs or the red light or the fact that Kiran and I had spent the afternoon unclogging the toilet after one of his model clients filled it with shit, I was jealous of Cavier's ability to just keep painting, despite the constant mess around him. I wondered, had I simply grown out of my first apartment, or had the Leaning Brownstone revealed the pathetic truth, that I wasn't cut out for the City or the artistic life, and for the long term, I'd need to live on more level ground? I didn't know at the time that I had Brooklyn apartments number two through five ahead of me, new constellations of roommates, landlord battles, plumbing catastrophes, different views of the Manhattan skyline. Nor had I realized that moving out of New York wasn't a failure of character. Or that plenty of people have found a way to make art without aestheticizing destitution. I've always had a hard time leaving places. It helps to have no choice.

I honestly can't handle the story of a dead dolphin, but that's what we have here. Mucky died soon after he arrived in the canal, and the necropsy revealed what we all should have known, that any dolphin who swam two miles into Gowanus was already confused and sick. That winter Kiran took care of me after orthopedists cut out part of my meniscus, and I did the same for him as he recovered from top surgery. We took our pain meds and turned the couch into a bed to watch *Childrens Hospital* on a laptop propped on our stomachs. College was coming to an end, and we were supporting each other as we limped over the finish line. I don't know how it took us so long to realize, but our landlord informed us that Cavier had barely paid rent all year, and we were all in danger of eviction. By that point, though, Kiran and I were both relieved to move on. In our last month, bedbugs ruined most of what we owned, we dragged our furniture back to the curb where we found it, and I dropped Samantha at my parents' place to give her the Connecticut squirrel-hunting life she always deserved. One morning, Kiran found Pilar dead in her habitat. Tarantulas were supposed to live for a decade at least, but this one had just keeled over. Kiran put her in a coffin made out of a cardboard box, but midway through the burial, Pilar's leg twitched. After Googling "is my tarantula dead" Kiran learned that to the contrary, she was in hibernation. To this day, Pilar lives on. Kiran is still writing horny poems, only he's now in Portland with his two partners. As for Cavier, he went on to become a well-regarded painter and photographer, his work selling for thousands of dollars, because the better the artist, the worse the roommate.

The other night I ran into my old friend Jorie at a party. To her friends, she introduced me as her former roommate, and it took me a moment to remember we had lived together for six months in the Leaning Brownstone. We ate South Brooklyn Pizza and drank Wild Turkey and took Klonopin. It was nice. It was easy. I had completely forgotten it happened. I've begun to think the point of a first apartment story isn't *look how far I've come* but *don't you dare forget.* I wish I could hold on to it all: every roommate, their pets and decorations, the taste of my terrible stir-fries, the burn mark in the couch from when the hookah succumbed to gravity, the Gowanus stink, Kiran's bearhugs, the modesty of our needs, and the enormity of our desires.

Believe it or not, the Leaning Brownstone is still upright. I make a point to walk past it whenever I'm visiting New York. From the street I have a perfect view of the fire escape outside my former bedroom and for a moment I return to the long, perfect hours Kiran and I spent out there along with whoever else was living with us. In the evenings we'd crack open our cans of Crazy Stallion malt liquor and have loud, excited conversations about whatever we were obsessing over at the time. When we talked about our writing, we'd say, "Well, Terry," as if on *Fresh Air*, which was both a joke and our greatest ambition. I remember watching the commuters stream out of the Union Street subway station, and sometimes late

at night we'd see a cab pull up and a woman and her little kids pass below our dangling feet and check into the
Holiday Inn Express next door. For a long time there was
a twenty-foot billboard on the north side of the building
advertising a memoir called *If Only I Could Sleep*, with
the tagline, "from molested to published." But from the
fire escape we couldn't see that, and instead had a perfect view of the brick warehouse across the street, and
the giant aluminum letters affixed to the front spelling
E-R-F-E-C-T. We dared not ask for more from a place
we were destined to leave.

DEAD PEOPLE'S STUFF

I was broke and needed stuff, which is how it began.

My sister, Charlotte, and I had spent the last three weeks driving our '99 Subaru Legacy from New Haven to Los Angeles, our route like an EKG betraying an elevated heart rate—Iowa City for bone marrow and watery beer, and in St. Louis, under a portrait of Michelle Obama, cafeteria-style okra, meatloaf, and fried corn, down through Memphis and the Lorraine Motel—no time for Graceland—a sci-fi-themed hostel in New Orleans, westward to Barton's Creek, cow shit on the windshield and baked beans in Amarillo; a jagged turn north to nude hot springs off highway 50 and seven-hundred-foot sand dunes in Colorado; our last day in Vegas we ate In-N-Out burgers animal style by a dirty swimming pool and made a special trip to an antique mall on the edge of the city where I bought a brooch that said "Bitch" in rhinestones because the next day we'd arrive in California, and our country, which had been as wild and welcoming as the breeze from the Subaru's open windows, was going to elect our first woman president, and we'd begin our new lives on the golden coast with the hot hood of our car crackling like wildfire.

In retrospect this was a bad plan. Moving across the country the day before the 2016 election was like driving a thousand miles per hour into a brick wall. I was in a fugue state those first weeks in LA. I'm told I slept on my friend's couch and applied for apartments (requiring proof of employment) and minimum-wage jobs (requiring proof of residence). The car got towed with everything we owned still inside it. Every day I got lost in another parking garage. At The Galleria, someone traced the word *MAGA* in the dust on our back windshield. A few days later, a black truck pulled up beside us at a red light and a skinhead straight out of central casting (after all, we were in Hollywood) leaned out the passenger window, tongue waggling. Eventually Charlotte and I moved into an apartment with our wrinkled clothes, and I spent an unspecified number of weeks flat on my back on a Craigslist mattress, miserable and paranoid, until one day Charlotte announced we needed certain possessions to make a home and we were going to this thing called an estate sale.

The sale was somewhere on the Westside—I didn't have a sense yet of where neighborhoods began or ended, and instead just punched in the address and went where my phone told me. When we arrived midafternoon, a procession of customers were already carting their purchases down the sidewalk to their cars. Old trees lined the block, that Los Angeles odd couple oak and palm. I signed a waiver at the door promising not to sue anyone if I tripped, and then a woman in a red apron beckoned me inside a house that looked as though someone still lived there. That would have been the artist Max Finkelstein, a minor celebrity in sculpture circles of Southern California. Along with his cutlery and furniture they were selling his last works, intricate Memphis-style patterns made of pink- and yellow-painted wood. His home was inviting and lived in, even as it was in the process of being dismantled by people like me.

This was a crucial difference, I would later learn, between an estate sale and garage sale. The latter sells possessions that are unwanted or spillovers—Christmas gifts you got double of, outgrown children's clothing. Estate sales, meanwhile, are in the liquidation business. Oftentimes run by private companies, the sales facilitate the complete clean out of homes belonging to the divorced, downsizing, dying, and dead. Give or take a family heirloom, an entire life's worth of belongings is up for grabs. As I was digging through the garage that was once Max Finkelstein's studio, I found half-finished paintings mildewing in the corner, sketches for future sculptures, pieces of balsa wood glued together and abandoned. It all felt illicit, as if I was trespassing and at any moment I'd feel a hand clamp down on my shoulder and Max Finkelstein would be giving me the bum's rush out of his workshop. But, he had died that August at age 101, a sale employee told me, and I should make sure to come back tomorrow when everything would be "priced to sell." Charlotte and I left with pots and pans, two side tables, forks, cereal bowls, half-used rolls of wrapping paper, and an antique patio couch that rocked on rusted Kelly green tracks. We wrestled the couch into our living room, a piece of furniture as out of place as we were.

After that we hit the sales almost every weekend—a hairdresser to the stars in Toluca Lake, a big-game hunter with a bit part in *The Temple of Doom*, a phone company technician whose house was filled with Rush Limbaugh books and a collection of carousel horses. We'd punch our zip code into EstateSales.Net and make the rounds, learning which companies encouraged bartering and the best employees to hit up for a price check. We had our own styles—Charlotte headed for the vintage clothing, anything with brocade or sequins, and I prioritized the kitchen drawers and garages. Together we learned to navigate the wait lists, guard the hold table, and master the lingo—a sale described as "Mad Men" connoted Mid-Century furniture and barware while "eclectic" was a euphemism for a grandmother with bad taste. Some companies spent months setting up; the merchandise had been meticulously appraised and dusted, price tags handwritten in cursive. At the slapdash sales, meanwhile, there'd be cabinets and cardboard boxes, sometimes entire garages, that no one had been through, and at those I'd find nude photos tucked in a drawer, or a rushed employee would have mistaken a vintage vibrator for an immersion blender and put it with the kitchen stuff. These were listed as "hoarder sales" or the inadvisably named "digger's paradise". They were claustrophobic madhouses but reliably cheap, as you paid for your merchandise in the labor it took to dig through piles of junk and moldy *Life* magazines. At those sales a miasma of panic and abandonment hung in the air, as if the home had been hastily abandoned ahead of a zombie outbreak. In my mind, scavenging through a dead person's belongings felt like a reasonable and productive apocalyptic activity. Besides, even the most depressing, ho-hum, picked-over sales had something to offer, and Charlotte and I weren't above taking home a dead stranger's old duct tape, door mat, bread knife, Himalayan pink salt, jar of assorted thumbtacks. How else do you build a life from scratch?

"Trash is created by sorting," wrote Susan Strasser in her history of American refuse, *Waste and Want*. "[E]very toaster, pair of trousers, and ounce of soda pop, and every box and bag and bottle they arrive in—eventually requires a decision: keep it or toss it." At estate sales, the first wave of sorting is usually done in advance, by the family and the company. The kitchen counter will have arrangements of china and Fiestaware, a hard plastic card table in the garage displays the power tools that may or may not work (the better sales provide an outlet and extension cord to test for yourself), and there's usually a glass case by the register with shoplifter-friendly items—pocket watches and silver Tiffany rattles, and if it's a union family, original Jimmy Hoffa campaign buttons, which sell out first. That said, no matter how meticulous the estate sale company, it's impossible to turn a house into a store, and as such, there's a certain amount of foraging that's up to the customer. Sometimes if you're digging through a box of greasy nails, they'll give out latex gloves. Mostly, though, you're on your own. Historians of trash like Strasser and Mary Douglas, author of *Purity and Danger: An Analysis of Concepts of Pollution and Taboo*, point out that while mundane, the act of sorting is a purification activity, and often takes place along the borderlines between the home and larger society. Garages, donation centers, trash cans, and dumpsters all link private and public life. Nowhere is that more visible than an estate sale, where a family opens their doors to the roving public to touch, gawk, sort, and thereby assign value to the objects that made up a life.

On the circuit, Charlotte and I became regulars—"the freckle sisters." We joined white lady boutique owners, mint-condition fetishists, scrap metal haulers, retirees, coin collectors, and my favorite, the nosy neighbors who buy nothing but touch it all. These were my people. We'd recognize each other across boxes of dusty action figures or half-finished sewing projects, not just by face but as fellow joyful warriors. It didn't feel like we were shopping. As events, they were less Black Friday free-for-alls and more like a cloud of eels and crabs picking apart a whale carcass on the ocean floor.

Soon, our apartment was furnished, but I couldn't stop. In a city of almost four million I had only a few friends, but each weekend I was beckoned into the homes of strangers, from teamsters to teachers to Jeraldine Saunders, a former cruise director whose memoir inspired *The Love Boat*. She died at ninety-five in Glendale and her house was full of romance novels, Ouija boards, and a framed photo of her appearance on *The Merv Griffin Show* alongside O. J. Simpson. Her obituary made sure to mention she dated younger men up until her death, and the author bio on her memoir, which they were handing out for free, reads, "Jeri Saunders...the vibrant, vivacious, and voluptuous Virgo from Glendale, California... and star of her own story!" Inside of one copy, I found a photo of Jeri and a hunky young guy. A note taped to the photo reads simply: "we were so happy!" I bought a Lucite egg filled with nails.

Then there was Jeanne Barney, cofounder of *Drummer*, a gay leather magazine for "the macho male." The line to get into her unassuming Hollywood bungalow looped around the block. One of the day's first customers (he must have camped out since dawn) left the sale brandishing a T-shirt that read Free the Slaves. I looked it up while in line: in 1976, the Leather Fraternity held a charity slave auction at a bathhouse, which LAPD chief Ed Davis decided to raid. Dozens of officers, a helicopter, and news media descended on the event, and forty attendees—thirty-nine men and Jeanne—were charged with violating an 1899 "white slavery" statute. (A year earlier, Chief Davis had sent a letter turning down an invitation to Pride Week, writing, "I would much rather celebrate GAY CONVERSION WEEK.") When Jeanne returned home from jail, she discovered that her house had also been raided. "I saw those cops had been in my house but you can't believe how torn up it was," she said in an interview. "They had taken my dresser drawers and emptied them in the middle of the bedroom. They emptied the laundry hamper. They had taken stuff out of my medicine cabinet and it was thrown all over the bathroom. It was a terrible mess!" I wonder what she would have made of the scene at the estate sale. Once again, her clothes were strewn across the floor; there were strangers pawing through the closets. Hopefully she's too preoccupied in leather Heaven to care that I took her paper cutter, set of poker chips, and a commemorative plaque, now proudly displayed in my bedroom, that reads "Thank You Jeanne Barney for M.C.ing the Mr. World-Wide Nude Contest."

The HOA tried to stop the sale at the Old Pasadena apartment complex, but Lester beat them from beyond the grave. In life, he was an estate sale regular, and all the old-timers in line had known him for years. "It was therapy shopping for him and then it became a compulsion," said a man with two beepers clipped to his belt. When he died, Lester was single, but determined to have an estate sale instead of let everything he had collected over the years revert to his hateful family. The HOA board fought the sale in court, but after a year of litigation were forced to accept a dead man's last wish. Lester's apartment was small and layered with antiques. We shuffled through in a line, grabbing what we could before being pushed along by the shopper behind us. The woman in front of me was Lester's hairdresser. She told me that Lester never had any money but loved to give financial advice. In front of us was a shelf of dozens of antique piggy banks, all empty. She picked up a military portrait of a beautiful young Black marine. "He never told me he served," she said. Under a Tiffany lamp I unearthed a black marble tray with two brass handles in the shapes of cats. I'm sure that Lester also found it at an estate sale. On the way out I walked behind a man with a camel hair coat, prompting the people in line to shout, "You better take care of that coat. I know that coat. Lester loved that coat."

Meanwhile, the block Charlotte and I lived on began to smell like death. "A cat died in the liquor store's dumpster," my teenage neighbor told me. Soon after, human remains were set on fire at the Home Depot parking lot. A motorcyclist was hit and killed by a Kia Soul at our intersection. It felt like people weren't just losing their minds but their souls. The stench got worse. "More dead cats," said my neighbor. Then one day I came home from work to find the city coroner pulling a decomposing body from the van parked outside our driveway. Charlotte and I stood on our apartment landing and watched the proceedings until the sun set, at which point I opened my computer and found a sale happening the next day. I was searching for some semblance of humanity, and I decided I could probably find it on strangers' bookshelves and in pine boxes of sweaters, in their personal collections (Yoda figurines, Victorian splatter glass, Kokeshi dolls, paintings of bathtubs), in opening an old woman's closet and trying on her church hats.

Unlike the rise of charity shops a century ago or the garage sale trend that started in the 1970s, estate sales seem to have been around, in one form or another, for as long as estates have been. For those wealthy enough to have amassed manors, land, art, and silk wardrobes, liquidation was always a last resort. Sale records were occasionally filed alongside the will and estate inventory, and in eighteenth- and nineteenth-century newspaper archives you can find sale advertisements, but never any coverage of the sale itself. And why would we? An estate sale is an act of undoing, and by its nature, resists preservation.

In 1984, a team of ethnographers made the documentary *A Country Auction: The Paul V. Leitzel Estate Sale*, depicting a sale in Juniata County, Pennsylvania. As the owner and operator of the last general store in a town of three hundred people, Paul Leitzel had lived at the center of community life. His store was a gathering place, as evidenced by the "loafing area," a collection of worn wooden benches that were reliably occupied by fox hunters chewing the fat in Pennsylvania Dutch. That is, until Letizel died and the benches, along with everything else he owned, went up for auction. "The family is dissolving their homestead, and in the process coming to terms with a death," intones the voiceover as we see footage of muttonchopped old-timers eating pie outside the sale. "All bid openly on the house and possessions, now exposed to public sale. In the process,

the personal, the social, and the economic, all become in-
tertwined." It's jarring at first, to watch this intimate community undertaking through the dry lens of academia, but
then, estate sales are born from the collision between private lives and inquisitive interlopers. Apart from the film-
makers, the outsider takes the form of a "notorious" antique
dealer from Trucksville named Joe Herman. His reputation
as a big spender precedes the sale. "We buy anything we
make a dollar on, and we don't let anything go cheap," he
brags. When the loafing benches come up on the block,
Herman easily wins them at thirty bucks a pair. After the
sale, one of the local men Herman outbid told the film-
makers, "I was bidding on them mainly because they were
of sentimental value to me, and I was really surprised they
brought that kind of money." He continues, "That's just
the way a public auction is. The man who has the last bid,
he's the successful bidder. But I really missed the benches
and the store… Because after you've been in an area and
went in a place like that for all those years you don't just
forget about it overnight." From there, the film follows the
benches as they're refurbished and upsold through progressively fancier antique stores, eventually bought for five-
hundred dollars by the interior designer for Sigma Nu at
Kansas University, so the fraternity brothers have a place
to sit as they wait for their dinner.

Agnès Varda took a more discursive approach in her
2000 documentary *The Gleaners and I*, which explores
France's fringe communities of scavengers. (Charlotte introduced me to Varda's work, and loves this movie so
much she got the poster image—two cat figurines in

front of a clock with no hands—tattooed to her bicep.) Then in her seventies, Varda begins the film by following traditional gleaners who, like those in the famous Jean-François Millet painting, collect crops from reaped fields, carrying away food "the machine left behind." This might not be as common a practice as it was in agrarian times, but Varda shows us that the *posture* of gleaning—stooped, eyes focused on the ground—is still among us. With her lightweight Sony DVCAM in hand, she roams the country interviewing those who glean for sustenance, for ideological purposes, for pleasure. We meet gleaners of grain, oysters, olives, packaged cheese, lost buttons, windshield wipers, even romantic partners, and of course the film itself is an act of gleaning, as Varda collects stories and images that cross her path.

Gleaning requires looking outside yourself, to the ground, the people around you, the dumpster, your interview subject, the estate sale, but invariably, your attention shifts back to your body, your empty stomach or grief or panic or decay. In *The Gleaners and I*, as Varda films her own hand, she narrates, "Then there's my hand up close. This is what this project is about, filming one hand with the other. To enter into the horror of it. I find it extraordinary. I feel like some kind of animal. Even worse, an animal I don't know… It's always a self-portrait." It's the same feelings I got at artist Michael Hogarth's East Hollywood craftsman. Hogarth made his living as David Hockney's framer, but his own work was rough and feral. In the living room I checked out his sculpture "Flying Rat Assemblage" made of rat bones and pigeon feathers fused into a kind of mutant animal crushed on Sunset Boulevard. There was an industrial trash can lined with plush cerulean satin called "Trash Can Coffin," and a collection of sculptures made out of kicked lighters titled "The Lighter Side." The placard description of those read, "These pieces were some of Michael's last work, constructed during the time he was going through chemo and found doing larger, more 'serious' work too difficult…" When I read that I felt my chest go tight. When dealing with remnants, there is always the specter of death, but as Varda reminds us, also the possibility of resurrection. When you feel yourself coming apart, just stoop over and collect the pieces.

Two years passed in California, and during that time I learned that the most depressing sales were the rare occasions when the homeowners were young and alive. You get the sense that these people need quick cash, and that by shopping there you're contributing to a legal defense fund. Their furniture is new and of bad quality, and everything has their original receipts, from the Pandora charm bracelets to the scratchy West Elm couches. "She originally paid 120 dollars for these sneakers. She won't let me go much lower," countered the salesman after I offered ten bucks, which we both knew was the accepted rate for a pair of worn running shoes. These homeowners don't realize that expensive taste isn't an insurance policy. Few things must be as sobering as subjecting oneself to the secondhand market, where people like me don't care that your HOKA sneakers are still in the box; if you're desperate enough to let us into your house, we already know we're in a buyer's market.

This was the scene at Rose McGowan's Hollywood Hills sale. It was just a few months after the *New York Times* published McGowan's rape accusation against Harvey Weinstein, and maybe it was a coincidence, but the sale was also Oscar weekend. In the sale description, the company wrote, "Just so everyone knows, she left everything here. So we're selling everything." There was armed security and a camera crew from *Million Dollar Listing*, and while the terms of the sale forbade members of the press, I suspect that most of the people in line weren't there to shop, but to gawk. The decor was a great mix of old and new Hollywood, an oversized RKO sign and Ava Gardner movie posters, a 2017 Porsche Panamera, an abundance of glass furniture and animal print. In the bedroom, McGowan's sunglasses and red-carpet looks were splayed out on the bed—a white tuxedo jacket, mesh pants—accompanied by 8x10s of her modeling the outfits on the step and repeat. It felt like an autopsy open to the public. There was Rose McGowan's Rosie the Riveter wall decal. There was Rose McGowan's Ravenclaw drinking glass. Pawing through a bin of scarves and tank tops, I felt like a member of the Bling Ring Club. They were selling signed copies of *Brave*, McGowan's memoir detailing her abuse in the industry. The sale, itself a fundraiser for legal expenses, felt like an extension of that project. As a matter of survival, McGowan was selling away parts of herself, and inviting the public further inside her private life.

At Johnny Depp's first wife's place in Valley Village
(Icart figurines and neo-Gothic furniture, mostly picked
over), I leafed through Norman Mailer's book *Of Women
and Their Elegance*, a tasteless "recreation of the mind,
the thoughts, the feelings, the *life* of Marilyn Monroe."
Alongside full-page photographs, Mailer bizarrely takes
on the guise of Monroe herself to recount a reefer-fueled
affair with a playboy named Bobby de Peralta O'Connor.
They fuck like mad, Monroe immediately gets pregnant,
Bobby's Doberman has his throat slit by one of Monroe's
jealous lovers, the pair attempt to murder Bobby's wife,
all Mailer's complete fabrication presented as insight. "We
cannot comprehend [Monroe's] inability to live with her
success, or her incapacity to make movies without tor-
turing herself and others around her, unless we are ready
to posit some awful secret in her past," Mailer reasons in
his author's note. "We can feel it beating in her heart—
some unquenchable horror, some incubus that lay over
all later success…" I thought back to this stupid book as
I bought Rose McGowan's Pikachu oven mitt. Why did
I ever think that by shopping at her sale, I would uncover some hidden truth about the actress? More likely,
the things McGowan loved, the possessions that would
have told me anything about her, she had packed up and
left with. Her real secrets were probably well guarded,
far away from the spectacle I was a participant in.

All week I had been anticipating Kathleen Nolan's
sale. She was the first woman SAG president, and an actress famous for Manifest Destiny sitcoms like *The Real*

McCoys and *Gunsmoke*. The sale was listed as a combination of Nolan's LA and New York estates: collections of Art Deco highball glasses, coffee tables made from railway ties, a "surrealist two-sided comedy and tragedy bust from the collection of Orson Welles." Just the sort of glamorous frippery you'd want from a woman discovered by Judy Garland while working as an usherette. The racist statue was so out in the open I didn't notice it at first, advertised alongside the Sheffield silver and telegrams from Lillian Ross. "Vintage Lawn Jockey from the 21 Club in New York" read the caption below a photograph of a crudely painted statue of a Black jockey, stooped and barefoot. Thinking there must have been an oversight, I alerted the estate sale company, and included in my email information on Dr. David Pilgrim, the founder of the Jim Crow Museum of Racist Memorabilia. Dr. Pilgrim describes himself as a garbage collector. For years he's scoured secondhand markets for everyday racist objects that served as a particularly insidious form of propaganda, reinforcing a white supremacist worldview each time you reached for the syrup or salt shaker, or in the case of a lawn jockey, walked through your front door. It's Dr. Pilgrim's mission to recontextualize hateful objects into educational tools. Each year the museum, based out of Big Rapids, Michigan, receives hundreds of donations of Jim Crow paraphernalia from all over the country.

But Kathleen Nolan's lawn jockey won't be among them. My email went unanswered, the listing stayed up. Halfway through the Trump presidency I should have

lost the ability to be disappointed, but after regularly at-
tending the sales I had come to think of them as a de-
parture from the ugliness of the world, and the people
who ran them as kindred spirits. But an estate sale isn't
an escape from humanity; it's a reflection of it, and like
Trucksville's Joe Herman, the companies that hold them
are just doing business. In the eyes of the bottom line,
the history behind an object is only relevant insomuch
as it adds resale value, and according to Dr. Pilgrim, the
market for Jim Crow antiques is booming. Of course
they'd sell the fucking lawn jockey.

Nolan's racism may have been on full display, but I
came to realize that at any sale, just behind the same old
Bakelite flatware, you'll always find the secret that breaks
your heart. At the flight attendant's duplex it was the
United Airlines internal memo announcing the wreath-
laying ceremony for his coworkers killed on September
11. At a pornographer's poolside sale, the dirty secret
wasn't the glossies of spread legs or the promotional dildos,
but the pornographer himself, now an old man camped
by the register and farting viciously. Sometimes the tragedy was as simple as a stack of kids' watercolors forgotten
in a vacant bedroom. Boxes of Dukakis and McGov-
ern buttons (mirroring my own collection of "I'm With
Her" merch stuffed under my bed). A decade's worth of
mother-daughter Weight Watchers material. Reams of
unproduced screenplays. A dog-eared copy of *The Cancer
Survivor's Cook Book*. In an apartment at the highest eleva-
tion in Silver Lake, I bought a terracotta planter covered
in clay figures eating each other's asses. At the same sale

I found a saved magazine clipping with a question from an HIV patient asking how to end his life. Did the house belong to the doctor who published his response or the man who wanted to die? Go to enough of these things and you can glimpse the shape of an entire life, from the garage of wedding china and dusty sports equipment, the pet hair and butt indentations on the couch, a hospital bed in the living room, the shoes in the closet arranged from kitten heels to loafers to orthopedic sneakers. Even the canes start out as bedazzled or inlaid but inevitably give way to gray plastic walkers stashed with the bedpan and half-used packages of adult diapers. In Topanga I bought a canvas sack of cowrie shells because they were a couple bucks and I thought their resemblance to tiny vaginas could lend itself to a fun craft project. After I paid, the sale employee told me that the late owner of the house had collected the shells on the beach in Vietnam as he served. I saw a teenage kid, far from home, stooped over a beach, gleaning. The bag of shells felt heavy in my hands and I just don't know what to do with them.

Somewhere along the road I stopped hunting for bargains and began searching for lives. I collected souvenirs from the dead like a grave robber, and I didn't realize what I was up to until an estate sale employee pulled a bundle of letters from my hands. "Oh, you can't have these," she exclaimed. "This has personal information, addresses and birthdays. Why would you want them anyway?"

From a well-appointed craftsman house I bought *The*

A.A. Way of Life, although I'm not an alcoholic. There was just something about the solidity of the book, unassuming and compact as a ham sandwich. The book's owner, presumably the lady of the house, had marked sections with such precision that she had highlighted the words individually and skipped over the spaces in between, as if she was processing each syllable as she read. In the section on faith without works she underlined, "If he does not work, he will surely drink again, and if he drinks, he will surely die," and at the bottom of the page, she had scrawled, "contrast to me as a practicing alcoholic—unwilling to be taught by experience—*'this time it will be different.'*" There was a set decorator who died in her fifties. I think given the chance, we could have been friends. I bought a curlicue iron plant stand, the photo book *Girl Culture* by Lauren Greenfield, garden clogs, soft pink bed sheets she'd patched herself, and for ten bucks, a 14x17-inch drawing pad. Each page is filled with bright, impulsive streaks of craft paint and Cray-Pas that could have been the work of a kid, if not for the diary entries scrawled in red marker:

Living in fear—economic fears, fears that I will never become anything. That I will never be able to support myself. I'm scared and I feel unsure; I am very angry that I made a decision that didn't work out to my advantage. I want to give up, but—

Bob and I just got in a big fight in the restaurant. I got angry at him because he licked his knife, and when I let him know that it bothered me, he did it again, and I told him it was rude and bad manners and walked out of the restaurant and didn't talk to him until we got home, where again I told him it was rude and he told me it was ruder to walk out of a restaurant.

I drew this after a phone call with my dad when he told me he preferred his friends at work, he got along better with them than his family, that they understood his jokes. I called him back the next day and told him that wasn't fair and he was hurt and said, "Well, I might as well know myself."

In Pasadena, I spent fifty cents on *Joan Crawford: The Damned Don't Cry*, a book made out of purple construction paper and magazine cutouts of Joan Crawford and advertisements for Lifebuoy soap. It's a punchline to an inside joke, the setup long forgotten. When I flip through it I can picture the birthday party where it was unwrapped, the whole room quieting as the recipient read each page with glee, the friend who had made it over his shoulder pointing out details. From the faint water ring on the cover, I imagine the scene later in the night, a cocktail carelessly placed on the book followed by profuse and drunken apologies. The next morning the crowd would have cleared out but the book remained among the torn wrapping paper and empty bottles.

The more personal an object, the less value it has to a stranger. What is anyone supposed to do, for example, with the photos? They're both useless and impossible to imagine in a dumpster. I started to save them in a scrap book with translucent picture corners. I have a series from one woman who glued commentary to hers, pre-Instagram captions—under a photo where she's holding a cat, she writes, "MORE freckles. MORE do. MORE chins." A candid sitting on the porch: "Even with the hair, does this look like a qualifier for Senior Citizen admission?" Polaroids of new houses and cars are common, along with military and wedding portraits, headshots, dogs, boudoir scenes, vacations. I added paper ephemera to my scrap book—a 1985 *Playboy* featuring the women of Mensa—"America's Smartest Females Pose Nude," a typewritten proposal for a television channel dedicated solely to cowboys. At home, my walls filled with amateur art—a painting of a disproportionate horse signed "Love, Grandpa"; a blasphemous engraving titled "Pope Toady and the Little Sisters of the Holy Pond"; chipped ceramic sculptures, tasteful nudes, a pop art canvas from a dentist that reads in groovy font, "Don't Squeeze the Toothpaste from the Middle of the Tube." If I believed in ghosts, my home would have been full of them. After years of estate sales the apartment became a shrine to deceased Angelenos. My cooking utensils held the memories of family meals made long before my attempts at shallot bucatini, and I ate my dinner off stoneware that may well have served a last meal. I ran errands in a dead woman's Uggs, sat in a chair scratched by someone else's cats, and wore Levi's broken in by mom butts thirty years in the past. My friend Lisa, who worked at the Met, once explained to me that when the museum displays religious artifacts they are intentionally deconsecrated. For example, in its fourteenth-century home in the Isfahan theological school, the mosaic mihrab faced west for prayer. In the Met's gallery, curators turned the mihrab east, in a sort of retirement from its original job. I was doing the opposite. On the daily I used estate sale forks, leftover Windex, wineglasses, pliers, and bathrobes, all in the same manner as their previous owners had in life. This all began because I needed a cheap couch and a few cereal bowls, and now I keep a scrapbook of unwanted family photos and houseplants that were potted by dead women that I've assumed the responsibility of keeping alive. Theoretically, I could understand why my generation retreated to algorithm-dictated minimalism— blank walls, direct-to-consumer furniture delivered in palliative shades of pink and cream, on-trend austerity, a style, described by Kyle Chayka in *The Longing for Less*, that serves as a "strategy of avoidance…when society feels chaotic or catastrophic." Personally, though, the last place I wanted to be was alone in a bare room with my thoughts. Eventually, I found long-term employment and friends in the area, but I still felt shaky and rootless, and I longed for the warmth of other people. In the words of the late set decorator who kept that sketch pad diary, "I want to keep going, afraid I might be over-stepping my bounds, want to do more, more, more, bigger, bigger, whole body effort."

A few years passed and I began to feel jealous of the dead people whose houses I was in. It's not that I wanted to die. It just would have been easier to have already lived a full and rich life with my potting shed and paid-in-full mortgage, and died of old age like Max Finkelstein, a few months shy of what felt like the beginning of the end of the world. The sales were evidence of a life that was once possible and now slipping out of reach. These people had crafting rooms, Oaxacan souvenirs, their kids' diplomas on the walls. They planned for retirement. Everyone had a hobby. This being Southern California, more often than not the houses displayed Reagan refrigerator magnets, Reagan commemorative plates, Reagan bobbleheads stored in the two-car garages. And now Reagan is throwing back jelly beans in Hell and his supporters are dead and dying, leaving the rest of us to deal with the mess they left behind, mountains of crap piled on countertops and stripped mattresses, a thousand times more stuff than one person could meaningfully use, to say nothing of the question of what we're supposed to do with it now.

At the end of a sale, things get craven. The clothing has been turned inside out and litters the floor. The remaining glassware is smudged with fingerprints. I once witnessed a customer try to dig up an orange tree in the backyard. Employees push leftover stuff in your direction, you lowball every offer, and across the frenzy, strangers yell at each other, "You can't afford not to buy it!" I know I've gone fragile, but even at closing time, I find it difficult to leave these places. Every house has something to give, and an accurate essay about estate sales would grow into a biography of every resident and an account of all their possessions and everyone who ever passed through their lives and left a mark, and to do all these lives justice I'd have to accidentally write the story of the entire world. A flash of recognition in James Agee's portrait of tenant farmers *Let Us Now Praise Famous Men*, where Agee laments, "If I could do it, I'd do no writing at all here. It would be photographs; the rest would be fragments of cloth, bits of cotton, lumps of earth, records of speech, pieces of wood and iron, phials of odors, plates of food and excrement... A piece of the body torn out by the roots might be more to the point." A bag of cowrie shells, artist's diary, annotated copy of *Our Bodies, Ourselves*, soup-splattered recipe cards, baby teeth, wishbones, collection of string labeled "too short to use." The archaeologist Ian Hodder has said that "as humans we are involved in a dance with things that cannot be stopped, since we are only human through things." That may be true, but the homes I remember best weren't the ones with the coolest stuff or best deals, but those that provided a blueprint for living. The people who had lived there had figured something out, it seems to me, and they wove their happiness into the everyday material of their homes—an anti-Freudian psychotherapist and collector of fertility statues; the first woman in Hancock Park to tear out her lawn and grow a native garden; Jeanne Barney, Lester, Jeraldine Saunders. At one time, Michael Hogarth had thirteen St. Bernards living in his East Hollywood craftsman. (He had a hang-up about neutering.) When I first moved to Los Angeles, I thought if I could spend enough time in these places, buy just the right keepsakes, uncover their secrets, maybe I could learn how to bridge the chasm between paranoia and camaraderie, hopelessness and comfort.

I've now lived here for going on six years. Charlotte and I no longer share an apartment, but are only ten minutes away, close enough to borrow each other's shoes. She works at a boutique where she sells clothing often sourced from the estate sales of glamorous eccentrics. As for me, my panic attacks have become as infrequent as the rain. Without underplaying the Lexapro, I've found there is no cure for loneliness like embracing a stranger's peculiarity. Inevitably, Agee failed to "write the whole of the universe down on the head of a pin," and he died angry about it. Personally, I'm trying to be content just to be welcomed over a stranger's threshold for a look around. I won't ever know these people. What a gift then, for every sale to still feel like a homecoming.

GROWING SEASON

Contractually, this book was meant to be

finished years ago, and it may well have been, if not for my garden. My husband, the budget balancer, hates when I say this. To his ears I'm confessing a fiduciary misstep, like investing in a time-share. The truth is, I didn't *accidentally* prioritize the garden over paid work, and if given a do-over, I'd make the same choices, only this time I wouldn't overplant the tomatoes. This is just the way it is. I spend more time in my garden than at my desk. By extension, this fiscal year I've spent more money on milkweed, terracotta pots, worm castings, etc., than I've earned, money that would only make it to my LLC if I quit mucking around in the planting beds and hunkered down at the computer to fulfill my obligations.

Any gardener would understand. In your little patch of dirt there are also obligations—endless obligations—to attend to. For example, as I write this it is late October, and where I live in Los Angeles, in plant hardiness zone 10b, my passion fruits are plunking to the ground and need to be collected and preserved, the peach tree must be cut back, the artichoke divided, the *Brugmansia* fed, the drip irrigation reset for winter, the bay leaves dried, the radishes, kale, broccoli, and fava bean seeds sowed. This would be my entire afternoon and then some, if it weren't for my other work, the work that pays the bank who owns the land that the garden is on.

When I was younger and lived in Brooklyn in zone 7b, I worked as a landscaper. It was good hard work, and I was very bad at it, although I tried. (Lesson learned: you inflate the skills on your résumé one too many times and eventually you'll look down at your hands and see a whirling chainsaw you have no idea how to operate.) Most mornings the crew would stuff the company's Toyota Echo with shovels and rakes and leaking bags of cement or mulch, or else carefully fill the hatchback with moist containers of myrtle, creeping Jenny, and clematis and be out in South Slope or Prospect Heights, laying slate, tending to the perennials. Each day I'd get filthy and misgendered. I loved it.

My first day on the job I had to assemble a backyard table in Ditmas. My boss dropped my coworker Mateo and me at the site with the hardware and a six-hundred-dollar slab of live-edge oak. Our job was to bolt the underside of the wood onto the metal frame. It was a misty spring day and I remember my knees getting wet as I kneeled on the damp grass under the table, diligently torquing the socket wrench until the screw was tight as could be.

Mateo worked alongside me and I could already tell from the soft way he handled the tools that he had been doing this work—actual work—his entire life. He grew up building cabinets with his father and uncle, and learned from them, he said. When Mateo asked who taught me I laughed in disbelief. It was obvious that no one had taught me anything. And also: *You, Mateo! You're going to teach me.*

I had worked through the pile of screws by the time I realized my mistake. There were two different sizes, and I had accidentally been using the longer ones. Like a dead man walking, I climbed out from under the table. I ran my hand over the surface of expensive wood and felt the slightest prick. A screw tip had pierced the surface, but just barely. Half a centimeter more and I would have ruined the table. I'd have been fired, or resigned in disgrace, then off to an office assistant job where I'd wear Ann Taylor shift dresses and be exhausted at the end of the day despite having done nothing. As it happened, I failed to ruin the slab. I kept the job and I suspect it changed my life.

"Natalie, are you feeling strong?" was the boss's way of asking me to lift something heavy, flagstone, manure, a contractor bag of gravel. He was built like a rugby player but was too pacifistic to ever play sports. He believed that a well-tended home garden was society's cure-all, and in every apartment he ever rented he'd rip out the concrete to plant whatever could take root in the polluted city soil. If my boss could have been turned into a tree himself I think he'd go for it, least of all because he'd no longer need to think about street parking.

Mateo and I built a fire pit out of river stones, laid brick, tamed a wisteria. I mixed cement with a short-handle shovel and poured the foundations for fence posts, and the next week we installed the panels which still smelled of pine and sap. We did bimonthly yard maintenance, hardscaping, heavy pruning. I heeled my shovel into overgrown backyards and found thick glass aspirin bottles, shards of porcelain buried in the soil. The blisters on my heels and palms burst then calloused. In my journal I noted "my biceps are intense."

I learned to arrange plants in waves instead of rows. I learned about transplant shock. We'd drive out to wholesale nurseries in Long Island and fill the van with compost, perlite, ferns, yarrow, goldenrod, coneflower, heucheras, juniper. I filled my head with new abilities, new words, some even in Latin. Most importantly, I learned how to put plants in the ground. Level the soil with a rake or sweep of your palm and dig a hole twice as wide as the root ball. Rap the sides of the plastic planter, tip out the plant, and tickle the roots to encourage them to grow outward underground instead of back into itself. Gently fill the soil in around the plant and pack it tightly to prevent air pockets. Water generously. Pack up your tools. Wish the plant luck.

Mateo was twenty-seven, the ideal age for a hot coworker. He came from Watsonville, California, along with 80 percent of the country's strawberry harvest. He grew up working on farms and later building fire-resistant homes in Central America, which is why he could actually do things, like speak Spanish and repair bikes and guitars and climb up cherry trees with a saw tucked in his belt, and which is why I predictably fell head-over-Timbs in love. What can I say? Know-how is a turn-on. Meanwhile I was unclear if to Mateo my chipper ineptitude on the job made me insufferable or kind of cute.

At the time, OkCupid asked users "Are you more horny or lonely" and while I would never pretend I wasn't both horny and lonely, more than that, I was desperate to *become* someone. If Mateo could love me—hell, even just like me a little more—he might teach me everything he knew. His abilities might rub off on me. I might learn to walk through the world as he did, as a person who knew how to handle themselves.

We worked day in and day out next to each other, up to our elbows in wet dirt. Mateo spoke with a stutter, and when he got stuck on a word, I filled in his pause with every romantic, thrilling thing I wanted him to say to me. I began to nurture vivid fantasies. Our van after a nursery run, a humid forest of palms and roses in the back, a bed of soil bags, our tool belts clattering to the floor...

While I avoided the six-hundred-dollar mistake with the table, each day I discovered new ways to fuck up. I ripped out an underground sprinkler with the lawn mower. I stained a slate patio with teak oil. My boss asked me to calculate a yard's cubic square footage and I came up with a number in the millions. I was constantly cutting up my fingers and shins and dripping blood all over the job site, which worried our clients. On a solo plant run, I got pulled over by a state trooper. "Did you know you were driving a commercial vehicle on a parkway?" he asked. What's a commercial vehicle? What's a parkway? There were so many basic things I had never learned. "Do you know how to use a tape measure?" Mateo asked me. I always thought I knew how to use a tape measure, but suddenly I wasn't sure. (I didn't!) I once drove the Echo all the way to Patchogue and back, only to have picked up the wrong planters. My boss yelled at me in exasperation and, ashamed of my incompetence, I heard myself offering to work the rest of the week pro bono. Behind my boss I could see Mateo shaking his head, trying to communicate, *Natalie, you rookie, never work for free.*

Over the season, my mistakes become less galling, although I never stopped screwing up. Eventually, I had disappointed my boss enough times that the experience no longer reduced me to a kid in the principal's office. The perlite stuck in my boot treads became the only work I took home with me.

The boring landscapes were for the landlords. They just wanted ilex hedges, red or black mulch, and new irrigation systems. When connecting the system to a power source, Mateo taught me to use special outdoor wire nuts. They each came with a little dab of gel inside, to protect the wires from hose water. This is how our city's infrastructure is held together, I was shocked to realize, by dabs of gel in plastic caps. When I walked around the city I suddenly had an eye for brown drip line snaking through the hostas. A person had laid that down and now the plants could live. It struck me that I didn't have the slightest idea how anything worked, or was made, or cared for. Every day as a landscaper confirmed that basically all my previous employment, with the possible exception of childcare, were as fake as the Astroturf we were hired to peel up and trash.

Most of our clients were Brooklyn creative types. I'd go inside to use their bathroom and clock the rows of Samuel Frenches, the advance readers, and Academy screeners, oh and what do you know, a row of Emmys or Tonys, shards of engraved crystal on the top shelf, modestly tucked away but still dusted and well-lit, stationed above the living room like the Chrysler eagles. If I ran into the client I'd nod to their bookshelf and drop some line like, "*Topdog/Underdog* really holds up," to let them know that just because I was cleaning their backyard I still knew who Suzan-Lori Parks was. As if I was the first person with a BFA to pick up a rake.

One day after work I was drinking a coffee by Greenwood Cemetery when a minivan pulled up in front of me. A middle-aged white lady got out and asked me if I lived in the neighborhood and if so how did I like it. She asked what I did. I was covered in dirt and wearing work boots and cargo pants with a pair of Atlas Fits sticking out of my pocket. "I'm a writer,"

I said. The woman whooped. "The artists are moving in!" she shouted to her husband in the driver's seat. She turned back to me. "Great news! We're buying a building here."

As much as the landscaping work rejuvenated my spirit, I couldn't ignore the fact that the people who hired us were new residents to neighborhoods like Bed-Stuy and Flatbush. They were almost always white and well-to-do and very concerned about securing the property lines. We'd rip out the chain-link and put up tall, tasteful pine boards. As they say, good fences make good neighbors. Hauling in potting soil, hydrangeas, and new picnic tables to yards full of crab grass and old tires, it was easy to pretend we weren't displacing anyone, and instead building something out of nothing. Everyone deserves outdoor space, I told myself, as if I was working for everyone. In a sense, I became gentrification's constant gardener. I replaced the cement with pea gravel, planted box hedge borders, and every two weeks the money appeared in my account like crocuses coming up through the snow.

The only part of the job I truly hated was the weekly house call to the heirs to the Purell fortune. It's not that they were cruel or unfair clients; in fact, despite the hours spent in their home, I rarely saw them. Together, three family branches occupied separate units on the tippity-top of a great glass condominium. (There was an issue, we were told, with birds breaking their necks against the windows.) To me, it was just too clean for comfort. Each week Mateo and I muscled our sacks of potting mix and buckets of tools past the doorman and onto an ear-popping elevator ride, arriving at the penthouse to lay our drop cloths and remove our work boots. Purell dispensers stood sentry at the front door to each unit. The Grand Army traffic far below was muted. Inside, there were usually other shoeless members of the help—the maid, the math tutor, the piano teacher. We barely spoke to them, and whispered among ourselves. Silence felt like an unspoken rule, as if our conversation was another kind of contamination we could track inside.

It is not easy to stay clean as a gardener. We were expected to move 100-pound potted plants in our socks. After pruning the Meyer lemon, we collected each leaf and twig and carried the clippings out with us as if evidence of a crime. When the wind slammed the patio door on my forefinger I silently caught the pooling blood in my shirt while I tiptoed to the bathroom. Each visit I watered the spider plants, which are known for fleshy roots and the "pups" that burst forth from the mother, creating a sort of hydra effect. In the wisdom of rich people, a couple of these hung above the kids' beds, and every time I watered them I risked spilling dirty water onto their sheets and pillows. Normally I could blame a mess like that on the family pet, but of course, these weren't family pet kinds of people.

At the Purell house I tried to keep my head down and my hands clean, but I was curious about these people who outsourced the watering of their houseplants. Why was one of the bedrooms only accessible via keycode, which I punched in every couple weeks to check on the bamboo? What was the story behind that canvas that read Godless Universe in glitter or the high-res photo of the couple posing with Obama? When I watered the oxalis in the living room, I'd stare at an art book with the sculpture *Supermarket Lady* on its back cover. The piece, made by Duane Hanson, depicts a housewife pushing a shopping cart stuffed with frozen dinners and junk food. The woman is made to look unhealthy and low-class because she has swollen knees and hair curlers. We are meant to understand that this is the bad kind of American. She has no taste. She certainly doesn't nurture fiddle-leaf figs in her home. But come on, she'd absolutely be buying Purell.

Mateo and I spent untold hours on the penthouse roof, defying nature to install a shrubby arboretum meant to shield the Purell family from the high winds. This necessitated lying on our stomachs on the hot wood deck to install an irrigation network under the floorboards, hauling up trees wrapped in damp burlap, sliding through the house with our boots in our hands so we could put them on outside and get back to work. One afternoon we looked up to see that the crew rolling tar onto the roof of the library across the street was scrambling to collect their tools; there was a storm blowing in, black, electrified clouds barreling through Bensonhurst and Sunset Park, straight toward us. Of course, all the little figures down in Prospect Park didn't have our vantage, and had no idea what was bearing down on them.

Winter arrived and I filed for unemployment. I knew

that for me, the job wasn't just ending for the season. I had lucked into it, and while I had won most improved, I knew my boss wouldn't ask me back the next year. I had to get real with myself. If it weren't for Mateo covering for me, I'd have been fired my first week. Even then, I knew that moving forward, instead of working as a landscaper, I'd write about it, and what a privilege that was; a job hauling stones all summer becomes an *experience*, just another anecdote to tell at the garden parties of my future. Still, I mourned the person the job turned me into. I had toughened up. I had garden-vision, and saw the world in chlorophyllic layers of trees and shrubs and ground cover, having learned the names of the plants I shared my home with. I watched *Jeanne Dielman* for the first time, and all I saw was compostable potato skin going to waste. My arms were toned and my ass stood at attention in my cargo pants. I could confidently operate a chainsaw.

I got to thinking about the deck build we did in a courtyard off Prospect Park West. Mateo framed the whole thing, scribbling measurements on the 2x4s with the pencil he kept tucked point down inside his hat. The slats were already cut for me, and all I had to do was nail them into the frame. Each board was supposed to be an eighth of an inch from the edge, and so as I went, I held up my measuring tape to the last board I nailed down. It was only after I had covered fifteen feet that I realized that I had measured a hair too wide. This is the kind of infinitesimal deviation that would never have been noticeable, if not for the fact that I measured each slat off its predecessor, and so as I made my way down the deck the gap widened into a chasm you could lose a hotdog through. Mistakes build off one another. I ripped out the slats and started over and worried I was in the process of making this same mistake on a larger scale. When I left this job where would I go if not back to my old way of living? My work would be climate-controlled and take place on the computer and there would be no time at all to sink my hands into the dirt. Every choice I made, from the internships I fought for to the film boys I dated to choosing to love this expensive city paved with asphalt that required so much effort to live in, took me one degree further away from what actually made me happy, the garden work that was now ending.

Mateo said he was heading back to California for the winter, maybe forever. He told me after our last shift, while we sat at the bar of one of the last remaining dives in Park Slope, where we could be among other people drinking whiskey at 3:30 in the afternoon. Jamaica Kincaid wrote, "The garden makes managing an excess of feelings—good feelings, bad feelings—rewarding in some way that I can never quite understand." Now that the gardening was over, I couldn't manage my excess of feelings for Mateo. The night before I had written in my diary, "I spent today gazing at Mateo's masculine forearms. He sleeps with lots of girls. Why not me? Well maybe because I'm his bro? Who wears work clothes and lifts heavy things with him? But if I don't make a move I will never forgive myself."

We split the bill. Mateo was going to Greenpoint and I lied and said I was also going to Greenpoint. The G train was late and crowded. We found standing room and I stared at his flexed arm as he gripped the overhead railing. The train picked up speed in the tunnel, lurching into the curves.

"So the thing is, I have a crush on you and if you were interested we could have a drink and make out some time?" I was saying. Oh god, this wasn't at all how I planned it. Mateo was looking at me as if I just told him I'd planted a bomb on the train. "Working with you meant a lot to me," I kept going. "You looked out for me on the job and never made me feel dumb, even though I had no idea what I was doing. And now thanks to you, I'm not totally useless. So I just thought, it could be fun to…have sex?"

Mateo was nodding now. Nodding in the affirmative, or in the way a therapist does to show he's listening? "Oh come on, man!" I shouted. Why wouldn't he say anything? "We were dirty and sweaty and spent the whole summer on our hands and knees in the soil! I couldn't have been the only one thinking it!"

Finally, he responded, "This takes balls." I was suddenly aware that three dozen commuters were listening in. I just hoped none of them would be that asshole to tweet the whole thing. The train came to a stop and I jumped off, not caring what station we were at.

"I'm around for a couple more days," he said as the doors closed. "Let's get that drink."

In *Life In the Garden*, published in her mideighties, the English novelist Penelope Lively writes, "the garden is to elide past, present, and future; it is a defiance of time. You garden today for tomorrow; the garden mutates from season to season, always the same, but always different... We are always gardening for a future; we are supporting, assuming, a future." I've tried my best to write myself back to those South Brooklyn gardens, to try to remember the licorice taste of purple Thai basil plucked right from the stem, the feeling of calluses, the prickly centers of corn flowers, because like gardening, memoir writing is also in defiance of time. But when it comes to plants, dirt, thorns, stones, summer heat, manure, there's no substitute to being there.

When I reread my diary from my landscaping days, it's page after page about my crush on Mateo, when now all I want to read about was my daily life on the job, those small, intimate moments with those gardens I won't ever return to. This is the unexpected sadness of that job; I never got to see the plants grow. Years after the job ended the world went into lockdown, and like many of you I nurtured a codependency with my houseplants— the tomatoes I sprouted from seeds my neighbor gave me, the pothos vines I trained across thumbtacks stuck into the drywall. The horticulturist Monai Nailah Mc- Cullough tells us that "caring for plants is the best way to learn how to care for yourself." Unlike the gardens I was paid to care for in Brooklyn, this one was mine, and all year I was able to watch my plants' leaves unfurl, tilt toward the sun. Those were the days when hand sanitizer was selling on eBay for hundreds of dollars a bottle, and I found myself thinking back to the Purell family and wondering if they were now watering their own plants. I tried to imagine what it must be like to live in a glass tower paid for by a company that only makes you richer and safer the worse things become at street level. Back when I worked there, my favorite part of the day was when we could leave and pile into the Echo to the next job site, one where I could curse, drink from the garden hose, and double-knot my boots. When weeding some overgrown postage stamp of a backyard, I'd push into the ground until I was up to my elbows in soil, and for lunch I'd eat my bodega turkey club with dirty hands because I didn't need what Purell was selling.

Like my old boss, the first thing I did when I moved into my house in Los Angeles was rip up rows of bricks in the yard. Underneath I found construction sand and broken beer bottles, but soil, too, which I've spent the last year building. I planted free shade trees—pink trumpet and crape myrtle—delivered by a city program. I chopped down the suckers from the Chinese sumac that were growing through the bougainvillea. I've begun to plant my own garden—milkweed, aster, dracaena, agave, moonflower, pomegranate, Mexican marigold, mallow, thistle, salvia Hot Lips, and for old times' sake, coneflowers, heucheras, and mops of sedge. I installed the drip line all by myself. I've done mostly everything in the garden by myself, and all without the secret knowledge that would have been bestowed unto me if I had ever managed to fuck Mateo.

(The final night we might have been able to "get that drink" before he left for California, I diligently shaved my legs for the first time in a month, wriggled into my tightest dress, and for hours sat in a bar next to the recording studio his band was using on the off-chance he'd have time to meet, which he did not. My flirtations became increasingly fantastical and deranged. I volunteered to help move him out of his apartment, and instead of being invited into his bed, I carried it down the stairs. The next day he flew back to the west coast and I texted him a photo of Guy Fieri posing with a six-foot-tall hotdog and then wrote, "oops wrong image," followed by a picture of my tits. My first ever sext. The next day, I woke to discover my thighs covered in pustulating sores—folliculitis, the urgent care doctor told me, from shaving with a rusty razor. The crush was never consummated.)

Today, I work out of my office which is in a small cinderblock room under the house. When the door is open, as it is now, I have a clear view of the garden. The fruit on my Buddha's hand tree is changing to yellow. The first sugar snap peas of the season have seized the trellis. When I look down, I can see a fine layer of dirt coating my computer keyboard, evidence of all the trips I've taken to the garden between sentences. I have hours—a lifetime, if we're being honest—of work ahead of me, but I also have cabin fever, and the all-consuming desire to dig in the bulbs—Georgia sweet onion, elephant garlic, daffodil, and hyacinth, because what else to do with an excess of feelings but give yourself room to grow?

WIFELINESS

I told anyone who asked, and often those who didn't, that I was becoming a child bride. This was a bad joke (maybe even, forgive me, a rape joke), as I was an independent twenty-seven-year-old, but I repeated it anyway, to my boss when I asked for time off, to my parents, even my fiancé moments after I proposed to him. Marriage at any age would feel too young to someone who never imagined she'd get married. I simply wasn't the type. I was too busy, too disdainful of men; I was the kind of sloppy killjoy who'd tell you to dump him and then later throw up at your wedding, and if I ever did tie the knot, I assumed it would be as a septuagenarian committing Social Security fraud. I was a lot of things—a terrible assistant, HPV positive, and I'd like to think a pretty cool bitch of a girlfriend—but me, a wife? Now that was a bad joke.

I met Chris—the husband in question—at a friend's going-away party. Right away I knew he was different than the other guys I'd dated. He had friends and employment, for example. He wasn't brooding. He was a good-natured, chubby hunk, with an orange bouffant that made him look like Irish Eraserhead. Oh, and he liked me immediately, a first in my life.

I was twenty-four and Chris was twenty-three, but he moved through the world like a dad on vacation and still does. When we go to the movies, he carries the tickets. When the cat kills a lizard, he disposes the body. Any chance he gets, he'll point his camera lens straight into a blazing sunset, always believing that this time the picture will come out. He's always fallen in love easily, with teachers, Kate Winslet characters, sardonic, down-to-earth girls who later figured out they were gay. Growing up as a nerdy ginger, he assumed he'd have few opportunities with women, and so as a kid he practiced kissing on a secret Barbie he kept hidden in his closet; this way when the time finally came, he'd be ready. The years of practice paid off; Chris is a great kisser, despite being the least-coordinated person I've ever met (and I went to art school). He is pigeon-toed and bowlegged. I saw him get peer pressured into a keg stand, and end up with a head wound. In the sun, his skin burns easily as rolling paper. A life-long indoor kid, Chris's favorite memories from growing up were the one day each fall when his mom let him skip school and together they'd take the bus into Manhattan to see a movie. Chris and movies, how can I even explain? He learned to read by looking up showtimes in the paper. He kept a scrapbook of box office listings. Name any movie released after 1996 and Chris can tell you what month it was released. Usually the weekend, too. This is how his brain marks time. For example, off the dome he tells me that the weekend he and I met *A Bigger Splash*, *Nice Guys*, and *Money Monster* were playing. And that when *The Accountant* was number one at the box office I moved out of New York, and when *It: Chapter One* opened a year later, he had just landed at LAX to build a life with me.

Within a few weeks of knowing each other we were in love and have been ever since. Still, for as long as I could, I resisted labels and commitment. To our friends, I described the relationship as just having sex and eating sandwiches. I refused to use the term *boyfriend*—so cloying and overdetermined, or maybe it had bad associations, considering that before Chris, I never had one. In any event, I called Chris my lover/roommate, which annoyed everyone. In my private, gooey heart, he was the love of my life, my honey bear, my big sexy marshmallow. My first adult relationship, I thought proudly. What a farce; we weren't adults! We were boss babies. We were horny make out partners in a parked car, about to get slashed. We were only at the start of the coming-of-age story, when you don't know who you are but everyone is still alive. And that's how it was with Chris for three years. We had the same friends and haircut. We split the rent on a one-bedroom at the intersection of Thai Town and Little Armenia and slept with a spray bottle under our pillows to fend off our cat when he made his demands at dawn. Life together was everything I ever wanted, as stable as can be that close to the San Andreas Fault line.

Chris had good work as a film exec, and was on his way to pitch a teenage horror movie when his mom, Mary Ellen, suffered a stroke. When I found out I left my office and camped out at a stuffy Beverly Hills restaurant. I ordered two glasses of their cheapest Chardonnay and a side of mashed potatoes with the idea that I'd sit there until a plan emerged.

Mary Ellen was once a wife, but when I met her she had been a glamorous single woman for a decade and showed no signs of stopping. In the '80s, she ran publicity for Springsteen, Dylan, the Kinks, and the Stones. She got married. She got fired for getting pregnant with Chris. She cared for her two boys as a stay-at-home mom in Montclair, and after a protracted divorce, she raised them by herself. After Chris and his younger brother, James, left for school Mary Ellen stayed in that big house with the family pets and stacks of novels. Her closet was full of night-on-the-town clothes—go-go boots, long black leather jackets—because all these years later she still scored backstage passes to every big show in the city. Like I said, unstoppable.

The first time I met Mary Ellen she took Chris and me out to sushi at the Central Park Hotel followed by the premiere of *20th Century Women*. At dinner she ordered for us and told us about rubbing elbows with Branford

Marsalis at Blue Smoke the other night, and recounted the time she saw the Mariah Carey movie *Glitter* only to realize she was caricatured in it, and how right then and there she marched out of the theater with her sons in tow. I waited for her to step away from the table to make a call before hissing at Chris, "Why didn't you warn me that your mom was a *babe*?!" Truly, in person she was one of the most beautiful people I had ever shared a table with. She had white-blond hair and upturned Brigitte Bardot lips and high, sharp cheekbones. "I've always been the husky ginger with the superhot mom, how do you think it feels?" Chris shot back. Frankly, I didn't feel terrific as the tomboy girlfriend, but I didn't care. Thus far she hadn't taken off her sunglasses, but it was still love at first sight. When I grew up, Mary Ellen was exactly the kind of woman I wanted to be. And then suddenly she was in the ICU, no longer able to speak.

Chris was on the next flight to Newark while I hung back with the cat. This was unfamiliar territory. Before Chris, the guys I dated were themselves the problem, and the only crises I had to handle were their personalities. Now I was unequipped for an emergency, and didn't know what to say when the news out of Jersey got progressively worse—a clot, a stroke, some tests, pancreatic cancer so aggressive the doctors had only ever seen cases like it in textbooks, and a few months—maybe a year but probably months—for Mary Ellen left to live.

"We knew that something was wrong, that the world was wrong (catastrophically), that we were wrong (catastrophically), that something (anything) was catastrophically wrong everywhere," writes Anne Boyer in *The Undying*. Like Mary Ellen, Boyer is healthy in one instant and dying of cancer the next. She too was a single mother, although when she was diagnosed she had the bad luck of her daughter being an adolescent. In Boyer's writing, she floods the world with iodine and reveals its sickness before us. With incandescent rage, her book enumerates the cost of her treatment, the insufficiency of paid sick leave, how she was forced out of the recovery room after her double mastectomy to make way for the next round of patients. "Everyone understands as a matter of fact that unless you are currently entered into this world's customary romantic partnership, or unless you have lived long enough to have raised devoted grown children," she writes, "you are, on the occasion of aggressive cancer in the conditions of aggressive profit, rarely considered worth enough to keep alive."

When Mary Ellen got sick, the structures and stopgaps I took for granted disintegrated like white bread in the rain. Who would care for Mary Ellen through her treatment? Who would rehome the family cats and dog, pay the gas bill, clean out the refrigerator, do battle with the insurance company, that after her one day in the hospital had already forwarded a bill for thirty thousand dollars? Mary Ellen had never remarried and had no partner. Her parents were long dead, and she was estranged from all but one of her siblings. Her younger son, James, was a strong, responsible kid who ended up saving her life when he realized during a phone call that she was having a stroke, but he was just out of college and in easier times, the baby of the family. So Chris stepped up, quit his film job, moved back to Jersey, and became his mother's full-time caregiver. I stayed back and wondered, at the end of this, who would be left for these two motherless boys?

I asked Chris to marry me over the phone. I had stepped away from my desk and stood on the fire escape at my office overlooking the parking lot. The building was air-conditioned and it was a physical shock to step through the door into the ribbons of heat rising off the asphalt. I was roiling with emotions, sorrow and panic and dread, and also love for Chris, the kind of adrenalized love that Christian mothers use to lift cars off their children. What was impossible became inevitable. Chris was twenty-six and had just gotten power of attorney. I was twenty-seven and had no power at all, but Life having just cracked my skull like a penny thrown off the Empire State Building, I suggested that we get married, fast.

The way I understand it, marriage once signified the start of adulthood. A young woman would live with her parents and maintain at least the illusion of her virginity until her late teens or early twenties, when practicality dictated she move out to become a wife, worker, mother. The oldest English word for a marriage ceremony is *bride-lope* or "bridal run," the tradition of an eager (or paranoid) groom hurrying his new wife home whether she likes it or not. Meanwhile, the Anglo-Saxon verb *wedd* means "to wager, gamble," because, since its inception, the institution wasn't about the relationship between the young couple but the one between the two families, an economic arrangement in the form of dowries, offspring, alliances, security. Even as romantic love became an acceptable reason to spend the rest of your life with someone, the wedding itself was still an opportunity for the community to celebrate its own continuation, and to cheer on the couple as they came out from under their fathers' roofs and fortified the ranks of grown-ups.

In contrast, by the time a couple ties the knot today, their adulthoods are well underway. We get married later, live farther from home, and very rarely will a hymen make it to the wedding night. In the estimation of sociologist Andrew Cherlin, a modern wedding is "a celebration of all that two people have already done, unlike a traditional wedding, which was a celebration of what a couple would do in the future." Fittingly, the weddings themselves are no longer community gatherings but lavishly produced expressions of the couple's identity. By this point in their adult lives, the couple has already figured out who they are and how as a pair to exist separate from the families that raised them. The perfect wedding just proves it.

Chris and I chose a date a month and a half away, when Mary Ellen had an off week from chemo. Her treatments were impersonal and agonizing, and the stroke had left her with aphasia, meaning there was a disconnect between the sentences in her head and the words she could say and hear. Chris lived alone in his childhood home and spent his days in the hospital or on hold with customer service, digging his way from under accumulating bills. One night Mary Ellen was awoken by two nurses in her room as they talked loudly about how soon she was going to die. Chris found her a new place to stay. On the weekends, James made the long drive up from Virginia. Their father flew in to help out. After all these years since the divorce, college, four people in as many states, the family was back together, but it felt fragile and temporary, like everything else.

Like I said, I never thought I'd get married and so I never planned my dream wedding. Under better conditions, I suspect we'd have just signed the papers at the courthouse and invited our friends to a barbecue. Maybe there would have been margaritas, mussels, and steamers. Butter for dipping served in mismatched Fiestaware. Vintage oilcloth covering the tables. We could hire a pizza truck with an oven in the back, and keep everyone hydrated with Foxon Park birch beer in glass bottles. I never watched *Say Yes to the Dress* and in white, I look like a corpse in a Victorian mourning portrait, but I always thought that if I felt compelled to drop some cash on an outfit, it would be a 1970s Paco Rabanne chainmail dress, the one with the clover-shaped sequins in mint and gold. We could play beach volleyball after the ceremony and at night anyone who wanted would skinny-dip in Long Island Sound, because we'd of course be at a cottage on the Connecticut shoreline—it doesn't take years of planning to know this—at the same place my parents got married in 1984 and one of my coolest cousins in 2016. The cake would be glazed donuts from the famous place in Clinton. I always thought envelopes of sea glass would make nice party favors. Not that I ever gave it much thought.

For our actual wedding, Chris and I improvised, and it showed. We had to find a place near Mary Ellen's rehab facility, and we ended up at an urban farm in Clifton that advertised itself as an event space, but until us, no one had ever taken them up on it. We forgot to refrigerate the Costco champagne. The flowers I ordered online and stored in orange Home Depot buckets refused to bloom. I had put the wedding on my Visa, and from the unlisted calls I had begun to receive, I suspected that my credit was flatlining. The morning of the big day, the news broke that a notable child rapist was found hanged in his prison cell before he could testify against all the other notable child rapists. I absentmindedly left the rings and vows in my parents' hotel room. The theme of the day was "fuck thinking we need to act" and we did and where it mattered, the wedding was perfect.

"To think only of oneself is to think of death," wrote Susan Sontag in her journal when she was sick with breast cancer and working out her book *Illness as Metaphor*. As it shook out, I never thought our wedding was about me, and to the extent I was thinking at all, I figured I could use my temporary social power as a bride to harness the energy around me like a clock tower in a lightning storm. I could be the conduit through which our friends and family transmitted love and togetherness and good tidings to one another, especially to Mary Ellen and her family, and counteract the tragedy we were living through. On the day of the wedding the farm was radiant with sunflowers and goats. Our guests arrived in polka dots, cowboy boots, corduroy, and mesh, all following the dress code—"brazen, sartorially courageous"—because this was a celebration of life, damn it. Mary Ellen wore a billowy pink floral dress, and when she arrived, pushed in her wheelchair by Chris's dad, I felt the anxiety of the day burn right off. Conviction settled in my chest firmly above my breastbone. In all its bluntness, marrying Chris was the correct course of action.

Hoping that the Quakers wouldn't mind some light cultural appropriation, for the ceremony we gathered our guests in a semicircle of rented plastic chairs and opened the floor to anyone who felt compelled to share. Our friends and family spoke beautifully, on our relationship and hopes for the future, their shock that Chris had found someone to love more than movies. I just wish that Mary Ellen, the one person I really wanted to hear from, was able to speak. When it was my turn, my hands shook, although I assumed I had nothing to be nervous about. Standing above the same baseball home plate my parents exchanged their vows over, I thanked our guests for looking so sexy and making it on short notice. "Here we all are, at a wedding that happened sooner than I ever imagined," I read from the paper I printed out at the Marriott office center that morning. "But everything that's happened in the last six months has taught me you can't ration your hours and days, biding your time for some perfect future beyond the horizon. And while we can't save our time, we *can* give it away to the people we love."

I tried to get at that galvanizing, queasy feeling of interdependence that came with love, how when Chris and I lived apart, at the end of each visit it felt as if he was taking my heart back with him through security at LAX. What I was reaching for—to this day still trying to get a grasp upon—was a retaliation against the illusion that we are separate. Insomuch as I have a belief system, it can be traced to a monologue in the fifth episode of the television show *Deadwood*. It's the funeral for Wild Bill Hickok, and in his sermon the reverend lays it all out there: "The body is not one member but many...the eye cannot say unto the hand, 'I have no need of thee'; nor again the head to the feet, 'I have no need of thee.'" The first time I saw this I was twenty-one and resting between training sessions for my college soccer season, which at that time in my lucky life was the most pain I'd ever experienced. It was preseason and I had just been made captain, and was hyperventilating over my challenge of unifying thirty-one girls into a single team. David Milch, the creator of *Deadwood*, wrote in his autobiography *Life's Work* that this sermon represents the purest expression of what he believes about us as a species. "There should be no schism in the body, but that the members should have the same care, one to another, and whether one member suffer, all the members suffer within it."

Through her education in pain, Anne Boyer comes to a similar conclusion realizing that few of us exist as just one person. "We cut each other open, leave wasted bits of DNA around, leave shards of evolutionary codices discarded in our lovers and mothers and children," she writes in *The Undying*. "Many of us have bodies that other people have sometimes lived or died in, too. It can hurt that we…are born into another sentient other's hands…born into the rest of the world, all capable of pain, too, which makes us hurt even more."

This was beyond my comprehension and likely inappropriate to read at a wedding, but maybe the day itself refuted the illusion of our separateness. That was my hope, anyway. After the ceremony I changed into white overalls and Tevas and we all ate pizza and danced at a musty Montclair tavern. By then, Mary Ellen was back at the hospital. The next day we dropped off buckets of yellow lilies, all the flowers that hadn't yet bloomed.

Everyone has a job to do in a hospital room, and as the new wife I knew I did as well. But what, exactly?

A month after the wedding Mary Ellen entered hospice care, and her room bustled with nurses and administrators in T.J. Maxx sweaters, all with clipboards and business to attend to. Chris and his brother and father took shifts sitting by Mary Ellen's bedside and in the hallway, on the phone still the task, carried out in whispered screams, of paying for it all. An iPhone propped in an empty Styrofoam cup played Sinatra's *Live at the Meadowlands*. At night we were visited by one of two women from hospice, both named Susan. After supplying Mary Ellen with lip balm or a morphine patch and making sure she was asleep, a Susan would sit cross-legged with us on the hospital floor and through quiet, frank conversation she'd try to ease our pain as well. The hospice nurses were attentive and unflappable, never without their duffel bag full of drugs and snacks. Everything you'd want a wife to be.

As for me, I surveyed the IV drip and funeral home brochures and worried I had thrown myself aboard a sinking ship. Witnessing Mary Ellen's final days felt like getting bundled into a time machine and forced to preview all the deaths in my future. The last time I was in a hospital, I was dressed in an Avril Lavigne costume. It was a couple years back and my friend had gotten alcohol poisoning at my Halloween party. As scary as it was to call paramedics to my apartment, I never thought her life was at risk, and the real terror came as I attempted to comfort her girlfriend with vending machine candy in the ER. At that moment, I realized that this was a full dress rehearsal for the actual bad thing. When my friend woke up I did my best to comfort her. "It could be worse! That woman over there had a disastrous wedding," I said, and it was true, the woman down the hall was wearing a bloody bridal gown. My friend groaned. "Nat, that's a Halloween costume."

What needed to be done for Mary Ellen? Everything and nothing. It felt preposterous that we all knew what was killing her but were powerless to stop it. I had been so fortunate, up until this point in my life, to have been spared a direct confrontation with untimely death. Until now, I had never considered that, in Milch's parlance, the one body we are all baptized into could be a sick body, a cancerous body. "In the industrialized world, an estimated half of us have cancer, or will get it, and most everyone, even if we don't know it, is carrying a little bit of it around," Boyer reminds us, even if I don't want to hear that shit. "Cancer doesn't even really exist, at least not as itself. Cancer is an idea we cast as an aspersion over our own malignancy."

A wife too doesn't exist until the body of her partner and the state make her whole, reproducing the form, failed as it may be. When I proposed, marriage felt like the sturdiest and most efficient way to protect a family from annihilation. Later, waiting for the inevitable in the hospital room, I wondered how that idea appeared in my head. The wedding and the six weeks leading up to it were one reflexive knee jerk. An unthinking emergency response. In hospice all I had was time to think. ("Absent action, all animals are sad," wrote Milch.) I thought, now that I'm married, am I different? Am I fucked?

When Mary Ellen was awake, she and I would watch re-runs of *Law & Order: SVU* or I'd read her updates on the Mueller investigation, because even in hospice, hope springs.

When she was asleep I sat in the corner with my laptop and wrote the proposal for the book you are now reading. I was coming of age, and in coming-of-age stories, a parent has to die. Their death has meaning because this is how a new adult is created, which is good for the economy. "In literature, one person's cancer seems to exist as an instrument of another person's epiphanies," wrote Boyer. "We are supposed to keep our unhappiness to ourselves but donate our courage to everyone." It was not lost on me that the moment Mary Ellen discovered she had cancer, she lost her ability to speak. About this specific essay, my book proposal reads, "it's a raw time in my life, but as always, I'm taking notes." As I wrote that I felt productive and unforgivable. In Lorrie Moore's cancer short story "People Like That Are the Only People Here: Canonical Babbling in Peed Onk," a couple's baby gets diagnosed with liver cancer, and the Husband tells the Mother, a writer, to takes notes, as they'll need the money from the story she'll write and sell. The Mother, loony with worry, refuses on the grounds that she only writes fiction, while cancer is grotesquely real. "This is irony at its most gaudy and careless," she says. "This is a nightmare of narrative slop. This cannot be designed." The real irony, the reader is meant to understand, is that the Mother's objections comprise the very story she's refusing to write. Are we meant to take this as an abandonment of her artistic principles? A capitulation to medical bills? It's true that the last lines seethe—"There are the notes. Now where is the money?"—but after taking and selling my own notes in a hospital room, to me Moore's story doesn't end with a principled victory or defeat, but ongoingness. The Mother writes the story because she is a writer. In moments of pure helplessness, we fall back on what we know how to do. Just like the other parents the Mother observes in pediatric oncology: "There is a kind of bravery in their lives that isn't bravery at all," she writes. "It is automatic, unflinching, a mix of man and machine, consuming and unquestionable obligation…"

I don't believe all sons would have done what Chris and James did for their mother. Their father, too, far exceeded what we expect from ex-husbands. Mary Ellen's brother and niece stopped by, my parents, a few others.

As for everyone else? Mary Ellen had friends, I knew this for a fact. I met one of them when she wanted advice on publishing a memoir about her career as David Bowie's hair stylist. Where were these friends now? I suspect some had slunk away. Terminal cancer has that effect. Others desperately wanted to be there, but Mary Ellen kept them out on purpose. She didn't want to be seen bruised and diminished. I understand; it's humiliating. We die alone, but with no privacy. Speaking, though, as one of the few of us in the room, we needed the cavalry. We lived off burnt coffee and pineapple cups. Even when taking a walk around the hospital parking lot, I couldn't escape the gluey plain rice smell of the place. Chris, his brother, and I took turns sleeping on a padded mat on the floor, the kind the staff used to prevent bedsores. Our caregiving efforts still seemed insufficient. I was too exhausted to be present and uplifting. Too green to know to take Mary Ellen's rings off before her fingers swelled. I sat vigil and surreptitiously Googled "what to say to someone dying?" An article on Cancer.Net recommended variations of "Everything is OK. We're here with you. You're safe," but we were pretty fucking far from OK, and I refused to pretend otherwise.

Meanwhile, the coward in me had a second thought: relief. Unlike Mary Ellen, I had smartly recruited a husband, and should the worst happen, I'd receive care from him that was consuming and unquestionable. To a coward, another person's tragedy is first and foremost an example of what not to do.

David Milch has his own sicknesses and addictions,

well documented. He's one of those Hollywood writers who would have died fifty times over—to say nothing of being able to produce work—if not for his wife, Rita. When they met, Rita was a film editor and fine artist. Her paintings now line the walls of Milch's room at the memory care facility where, at age seventy-seven, he's being treated for Alzheimer's. To be sure, losing his faculties is a demoralizing elephant fuck—his words—but for Milch life carries on through writing projects and family life, which he's succeeded in braiding together. He wrote his memoir in collaboration with his daughters and Rita, who over the decades ensured that Milch's TV writing sessions were recorded and transcribed. When a reporter for the *New Yorker* visited their house in 2019, boxes of these transcripts filled the floor of Rita's art studio. Milch still believes in the essential oneness of the human spirit, but in his final days that idea finds its expression not in the wide outside world but in those closest to him. "I still hear voices. I still tell stories. There are those in my head and another in my throat and others in my work. There is the voice in my wife's head and the ones in my children's heads," he writes. "The deepest gift I think an individual can experience is to accept himself as part of a larger living thing, and that's what we are as a family."

Family life requires a different calculation for women. "I had quit writing for years, and then when my daughter was small and I was in an abusive relationship and I had to get out and I just wanted to die and I decided to write poetry again and it saved my life," said Boyer in an interview for the Commonplace podcast. But a few years after leaving her bad relationship, Boyer undergoes cancer treatment while single, without a partner's salary or health insurance, or his consuming and unquestionable obligation to her care. Partnered or unattached; what road to take when either can kill you?

Milch admits that he was often a terror to his wife. He'd sell off their furniture for drugs, used heroin when the kids were young. When Rita was in labor with their first child, Milch was on the phone buying a racehorse. "Not enough action in the room for you, Dave?" she said from the hospital bed. Later, he kept his gambling relapse a secret until Rita discovered the family was seventeen million dollars in debt, a pit she's been digging them out of ever since. When I read this, it's easy to project the role of stifled caregiver onto Rita. Sure enough, it's a common story, but the only problem is, Rita isn't the one telling it. Unlike her husband, her work and inner life has not been the subject of decades of critical analysis. She has not published a memoir.

Chris is a born wife guy. He bought himself a heavy platinum wedding band. (Mine is sterling, twenty-five bucks from a Montclair jumble shop.) He loves to refer to me as his wife, especially among new people, as in, "excuse me, this hamburger is actually for my *wife*." He aspires to be Stan in the last episode of *Mad Men*, massaging Peggy's shoulders as she works. In fact, as I write this, he's in the kitchen listening to one of his movie-ranking podcasts and cooking me a quesadilla.

Which of course makes my unease about married life a special level of bitchiness. It's just, I've done the reading.

Statistically, marriage isolates and stultifies, and research shows that for women, the institution dampens political activism and erodes friendships. The modern expectation is that a couple achieves total self-sufficiency—social, emotional, financial, sexual. An island nation of two. Despite arming myself with this foreknowledge, after I became a wife I still felt that inexorable drift inward. Chris and I had planned on taking a vacation in Italy, but it was winter 2020 and so instead we honeymooned in lockdown. Housebound, I felt reduced to my marital status. The horizon of my days narrowed to the size of our one bedroom, the dirty litter box, mung beans soaking overnight for tomorrow's dinner, a day that would be just like this one only with different food and worse headlines. With each meal for two I cooked I sank further into my new station, one half of a whole, like a lung, perpetually making myself useful. As if to match my new matronly station, my body significantly changed during this time. As soon as our marriage license arrived in the mail, I became buxom, as pillowy as a soup dumpling, which was a real issue for someone whose entire wardrobe was button-down shirts. That said, if there's one good use for a bosom it's to hold your grieving husband's face against as he cries for his mother, and in that respect I found myself equipped. Wives are designed, I learned, to embody the solutions to other people's needs.

As isolating as lockdown was, Covid stripped away the last bits of veneer off the lie that human lives are separate, our fates our own. The plague magnified my personal struggles seven billion times over. Our grief and numbness was everyone's grief and numbness. Mothers were dying all over the place. We were all simultaneously confronted by our elephant fuck of a for-profit healthcare system. As I worried that I'd someday be kneecapped by the marriage I'd just made official, everyone in the world was trying to survive a disease that was spread by those closest to us. Simultaneously, we all realized that despite the danger of contamination, we needed each other, for care, mutual aid, counteroffensives, sanity, love, fellowship, casseroles.

Before the plague, when our family's suffering was a private catastrophe and we had all spent a week in a hospital room counting breaths, I suggested to Chris that he go out to dinner with James and their father to get some air and discuss next steps. They would only be gone a couple hours. I'd keep watch as Mary Ellen slept through their absence.

They left, and I sat in a chair by the window. The sun set, and in the room's darkness I failed to notice Mary Ellen had woken up. She stepped out of bed to take herself to the bathroom, forgetting she could no longer walk. I leaped up and dashed around the bed to help her, but I was a step too late, and we both ended up sinking to the floor in each other's arms. My mother-in-law cried out in pain. I yelled for a nurse to come help, but no one answered.

I was stuck on the hospital floor with my arms wrapped around Mary Ellen. Finally, here is what it was all for, adulthood. And I still didn't know what to do, alone with a dying person. I tried to gently lift her back into bed, as I imagined the hospice Susans or my own parents or Olivia Benson would do, but I wasn't strong enough to be graceful and too tentative to be effective. I still wanted to maintain the barrier between us. She was the matriarch, self-assured, sovereign. I was a lightweight, just a girl her son was into. But that wasn't the way things were anymore. I scooped Mary Ellen up, firmly this time. She yelled in pain, and as I lifted her off the floor I saw under her hospital gown the caesarian scars on her stomach from when she gave birth to Chris. Then she was back in the safety of the bed and she curled up in the sheets and cried until she fell asleep and I hovered over her and rubbed her back and waited for the rest of the family to return.

When the revolution comes, we won't need wives anymore. Caring for Mary Ellen wouldn't fall to just her sons. Treatment will be free and deprivatized. Cancer itself won't exist as we know it today, the carcinogenosphere extinguished along with the industries that feed it. As it stands though, pancreatic cancer has no cure. "Mortality is a gorgeous framework," writes Boyer, now as cancer-free as one can be living in the world as it is. Unlike Mary Ellen, she was able to walk out of the cancer ward, ecstatic that she gets to live, and not as a "subtle or delicate person whose inner experiences are made only of taste and polite feeling...while all the rest of the world always, really, actually bleeds." We can reject the pablum, I hope, that a sick woman is, in Boyer's words, the "angel of epiphany," while still learning a thing or two. As Milch looks back, he writes, "the truth comes home that this life is real and it's earnest and it's for all the marbles... The least desirable of all possibilities is to die stupid, to die without having recognized what's at stake." Or as the head of Palliative Care at Mt. Sinai told the *New York Times* during the height of Covid deaths, "Meaning comes through relationship. The fear of death is about the loss of relationship with the world and the people in it." In my desperate, insufficient, fullhearted way, I did my best to build more relationships—husband, in-laws, a rallying of friendships. I turned myself into a wife, which is another way of saying an adult or a human shield.

The next night Mary Ellen died. In the hospital room, her survivors hugged and drank more coffee. When the funeral home people arrived they brought a body bag made out of carpet instead of black plastic, a nice touch. Once again, I felt unprepared for the moment, that old nightmare of forgetting to study for an algebra test. I busied myself coordinating with the nurses and clearing away our half-eaten Clif bars, flitting from task to task as quietly as possible because it seemed rude to flaunt my alive-ness in front of a dead body. I admired Chris for his ability to cry, even as I wished I knew how to console him. That's just the way Chris has always been; he makes loving look easy. Months later, Chris would write a remarkable essay about his mom and the movie *Joker*, which opened the week she died.

My *JOKER* viewing was always going to serve as a sort of private exorcism. A clumsy stroke at [adolescent boy] heart strings which I happily discovered no longer resonated in my moviegoing heart… When I was a boy, there seemed to be nothing more meaningful than art about rage, pain, and misery. Yet having served as a caretaker, the fraudulence of a film about the indignity of a man having to serve as his mother's caretaker could not have made itself more apparent. And in this moment of pain, I remembered how much of that past summer had been spent with my mom in laughter, frustration, exhaustion, and a strange sort of prevailing contentment...

The day of the funeral, I was walking down Broadway dressed in my bereavement slacks and struggling to carry a heaping bouquet of lilies when a cabbie leaned out his window and shouted, "Smile, honey!"

"I'm on my way to a funeral!" I shrieked back.

"Smile 'til you get there!" he said as he drove off.

That last night at the hospital, as we waited for the paperwork, I thought about how the difference between a very sick person and a dead person is so stark that even a nonbeliever like me would have to accept the tangibility of a soul. If souls don't exist how else could I explain Mary Ellen's sudden disappearance? The last place I wanted to be was in the room with the body, but the nurses told us that the final thing to go is a person's hearing, and even though Mary Ellen's heart had stopped beating, we should keep talking to her. I tried my best not to be afraid. "Everything is OK. We're here with you. You're safe," I told her, because it never ends, our obligation to care for one another.

BIG TROUBLE
IN LITTLE VAGINA

So I woke up and decided that over the course of the day I'd have twelve donuts, eighteen beers, and twenty-four orgasms. I'd have to walk six miles, too, probably while drinking Tecate Light out of my water bottle.

"I just want to let you know that I'm going to come twenty-four times today," I alerted my husband, Chris.

The night before we had gone to a networking event disguised as a birthday party. There were too many rich kids and so little food and that morning we were both hungover from sparkling Syrah. Chris rolled out of bed and put on a pot of coffee. This was our dynamic. In the movie version Chris would be played by Stanley Tucci in his most supportive husband role to date.

It was 10:35 a.m. Pacific Standard Time. Over the next twenty-four hours I'd push my body to the limits of gluttony. In two weeks I was turning thirty but that morning I felt as exhilarated and pathetic as I did in my midtwenties, when I first heard about the 6, 12, 18, 24 challenge.

"Have you heard of the 6, 12, 18, 24 challenge?" asked Cody, my only straight male friend. This was years ago, back during the second Obama administration, and we were day drunk at the neighborhood bar which was also a bowling alley. I told Cody to save the brain teaser shit for his students—he taught AP calc—but he said if he brought up the 6, 12, 18, 24 challenge at school the PTA would publicly hang him. It was a frat dude test of endurance, he explained, in which participants had twenty-four hours to finish four distinct tasks, one six times, one twelve times, one eighteen times, and one twenty-four times; the breakdown was up to you and the categories were: donuts consumed, cans of beer drunk, miles either run or walked, and jerk-offs to completion. And yes, I was confused at first, too. To rephrase, out of donuts, beers, miles, and solo orgasms, you decide which one you do six times, which one twelve times, and which ones you grind out eighteen and twenty-four times, all in a calendar day. Back at the bowling alley I chewed it over. I asked the bartender for a pen and scratch paper, feverishly crunched the numbers. Like algae in a warming sea, obsession bloomed in my chest.

Learning about the 6, 12, 18, 24 challenge is like

watching the VHS from *The Ring*, which means if you're reading this it's already too late. At first talking about the game seems like just another way to shoot the shit with friends. But soon your pulse quickens—you can't change the subject even if you wanted to, and a vision appears, there you are in the not-too-distant future, dusted with a benediction of donut crumbs and applauded by a crowd of loved ones, having just conquered the challenge and by doing so, won immortality. Back in the present, you wonder…what if? Could I? But how?

Later that night at my apartment, over a spread of pupusas and Rolling Rock, I threw the challenge to my larger group of friends. At the time I was just another single white female. My Tinder profile read "Brooklyn's newest lettuce farmer," and I dated a loose affiliation of jabronis in the hopes of getting fucked, which I managed to do only occasionally. In one sense I was desperately lonely, but I wasn't alone, not by a long shot. I had a crackerjack group of best friends from college, and childhood friends from New Haven, like Cody, moving to the city each year. Together we drank and schemed and lent each other the same twenty dollars, depending on who was most broke that week. On Sundays Elaine and I would try and fail to sell our wardrobes at Beacon's Closet, and then soothe our egos with happy hour white wine, trash bags of unsold clothes at our feet. Kim was a terrific cook and would whip together big pots of shakshuka or taco pasta anytime of night, and each July I'd throw an obscenely irresponsible Independence Day party at my grandfather's vacant house in Old Lyme, where we'd play gays-v-straights volleyball and wade black-out drunk in Long Island Sound. After my shift at the lettuce greenhouse, I'd spend each night with one configuration or another of this friend group—planning road trips we'd never go on, snacking, watching Colin Farrell's sex tape. And while it was true that just about every last stinking one of them was in a serious relationship, why would I mind seventh-wheeling when that meant I was surrounded by six people who loved me?

My friends and I spent that night breathlessly debating the 6, 12, 18, 24 challenge, each of us passionately committed to our chosen strategy. Always the math teacher, Cody calculated that with the assumption he'd take six hours to sleep, he'd have to maintain a completion rate of 3.33 tasks per hour, which he'd approach methodically, scheduling beer and donut rest stops over the course of an eighteen-mile run. Kiran planned to start his day in the Bronx and walk all the way to South Brooklyn, arguing that the slight topographical decline would give him an advantage completing miles. Elaine was in her Health Goth era, and was counting on hydration and B5 vitamins. Some were convinced that the only way to get the jump on this thing was to blitz it—power through the categories as fast as possible until the pain caught up with your body. My personal philosophy was that while it seemed as though the categories were designed to inflict maximum discomfort, you could, in fact, achieve balance: donuts absorb beer, running burns off donuts, beer lowers orgasmic inhibitions, and orgasms invigorate the spirit.

From the jump, my breakdown was always: six miles

(blame it on my busted meniscus), twelve donuts, eighteen beers, and twenty-four orgasms with a bullet. The orgasms were the whole point. Without the orgasms, this was gross. With the orgasms, poetry. The cis guys had different plans for every category except the jerk-offs. Out of biological necessity, they all agreed, the jerk-offs simply had to take the six spot. And to think, these mayflies are the people running our governments! The 6, 12, 18, 24 challenge was designed by men, popularized by the rape advocates over at *Barstool Sports* (more on them later), and yet in an elegant turn, it favors women—really any of us with a clit, and the capacity to die a little death and resurrect oneself again and again and again, onward to victory. As a concession and a flex, the girls in the group decided we wouldn't count multiple orgasms in a single session, and would need to come and then take a beat before starting up again. As if something as insignificant as a refractory period could stop me! A playwright friend told me that the 6, 12, 18, 24 challenge would be my version of a Marina Abramović piece. I thought of it in terms of Patrice O'Neal's ejaculation joke: "We both have orgasms, but men have a *receipt*... You don't think you'd be happier, ladies, if you could just shoot a couple of eggs in a guy's face, right on top of his forehead?" The 6, 12, 18, 24 challenge was my money shot. If the single men of New York had no interest in partaking in my orgasms then they would have to be bested by them. I wanted them (who? Everyone!) to look upon my works and despair.

Obviously, we had no choice but to plan a group attempt. We'd pick a holiday weekend. Order "Dirtbag of the Year" commemorative plaques. Update each other on our progress throughout the twenty-four hours in a group chat that would either be published or destroyed. And when the day came to a close, we promised to converge at our favorite bar next to Greenwood Cemetery and finish our last beers together, toasting our unyielding commitment to the bit.

Beyond foggy memories, all that remains of my 6, 12, 18, 24 challenge attempt is the notebook where I recorded my progress like a captain's log. Reading through the entries, you could see the day began languidly. Morale was high. I had dessert for breakfast and a fleet of vibrators charging by my bedside.

11:15 a.m.
Chris brings me two glazed donuts. I eat them in bed while reading a blog about garden composting. I've come three times. Decadence.

11:33 a.m.
Brought out the Hitachi. I came easily but at what cost? 20 to go. Should I be worried about sanding my clit off?

11:50 a.m.
Cracked a Tecate Light in the yard. I wanted to cut some logs with the chainsaw, but it's out of oil. Couldn't relate.

Five years ago, when my friends and I were coordinating our group attempt, it was a challenge finding a time that accommodated the work schedules of an executive assistant, urban farmer, grad student, PA, and high school teacher (not to mention our second jobs as tutors, free-lance writers, and babysitters). We never found a date. Then I met Chris and I moved across the country, and soon the concerns of my twenties began to feel just as far away. I no longer worried about bedbugs or getting scammed by a Craigslist job listing or a first date reading aloud his screenplay at happy hour. Time had domesticated my anxieties. Melanoma. Car payments. Health insurance for dogs. I was no longer a minimum wage lettuce farmer, and it didn't matter that my attempt at drinking eighteen beers spilled into Monday morning because I worked for myself, a very forgiving employer. The morning I began the challenge, Chris and I watched our elderly dog poop on the neighbor's cactus and had a laugh about the party we had been to the night before. We met one guy who aspired to make a version of *Chef's Table* where the food would look inedible. "That's reality," he explained. That walk was supposed to be my first mile of six, but unfortunately it was a 90-degree November day, and our dog, who had just lost an eye to glaucoma, insisted on heading home before I banked even half a mile.

12:35 p.m.
Cracked my second beer. Starting Three Days of the Condor *with Chris.*

1:10 p.m.
Seventh jerk-off. Anxious about performance anxiety tbh.
Probably easier to bank orgasms when I was sexually mis-

erable. I'm understanding this is a challenge meant for someone with nothing to lose.

Back when the 6, 12, 18, 24 challenge entered my life, the worst problem I could fathom was mankind continuing to not want to have sex with me. Since adolescence my interest in sex had outweighed my participation in it. As a tenth grader, I was a member of STARS (Students Teaching About Responsible Sexuality) at my local Planned Parenthood, where I was trained in everything from consent to testicular anatomy, handed a tote bag full of condoms, and dispatched to my high school to make up for the statewide lack of sex ed. I foisted dental dams on all my classmates, and would remain a virgin for another six years. In college, I decided to write about the sex I wasn't having. For those who argue personal essay is a masturbatory genre, you'll feel vindicated to know that the first assignment I turned in to my nonfiction class was called, "83 Ways to Begin a Vibrator Essay," and it was just that—a list of 83 possible first sentences for an essay about my first vibrator.

- *My new vibrator looks less like a sex toy and more like a kitchen gadget from IKEA.*

- *After watching a documentary on female genital mutilation, I stopped taking things for granted.*

- *We buy ourselves vibrators in order to live.*

- *This story is not about loneliness.*

- *This story is not yet about loneliness.*

And so forth and so on. My big formal idea was that each subsequent line represented a revision, dramatizing a writer (me) struggling to explain the meaning of her vibrator. In my defense, I was twenty. I had recently learned to jerk off and was furious I had wasted so many years not jerking off. Me not coming for two decades felt like the designs of a far-reaching conspiracy.

A short time later I finally had sex in an NYU frat apartment on Avenue C. Inexplicably, his bedroom walls were covered in corrugated tin, giving the impression I was getting penetrated in a shipping container. I think I climaxed from the sheer relief of not being a virgin anymore—*oh god, at last!* Afterward he brushed the hair from my face, lowered his lips to my ear, and whispered, "I'm not looking for a girlfriend right now."

Whenever anything happened to me I told all my friends. I'd go to Elaine first, because she was the hottest and most maternal. We had met in screenwriting class where Elaine wrote about girls fixing muscle cars despite not knowing how to drive herself. She had billowy *Moonstruck* hair and being the oldest of three sisters, she taught me how to give a blow job and format my résumé. Elaine had a mind full of filth. She introduced me to sports sheets, Babeland, and at Ren Faire (Elaine was a freak for Ren Faire), she interrupted a falconry demonstration to add, "If this guy can control a bird like that, imagine what he can do with a *pussy*!" Her one vice was WebMD. She was always convinced there was something amiss in her body, and her anxiety manifested in a vortex of Zocdoc searches and hastily scheduled biopsies. I held her hand through an emergency visit to the OB-GYN, and likewise, she was always there for me when I felt particularly undateable. I'd burst into her apartment in tears; she'd toss her Swiffer aside, and exclaim, "Little buddy! What's the problem?"

Clearly, I was the problem. In private, I thought of myself as Quiz Kid Donnie Smith from *Magnolia*, a depressive with so much love to give and nowhere to put it. Back when I was a virginal sex educator, my class presentations always began with an ice-breaking game called "Pleasures and Dangers." In a circle we'd toss around a beach ball and crowdsource a pros and cons list for sex. Pleasures: romance, orgasms, pregnancy, burns calories. Dangers: revenge porn, pregnancy, damnation, yeast infections, herpes. You get the gist. The exercise was meant to illustrate that it was easier to name dangers than pleasures because we'd all been conditioned to associate sex with violence, shame, and pubic lice. But over the years I ran this exercise and urged my peers to shout out every possible consequence from Doing It, no one ever considered that desire unfulfilled was a danger all its own. I was terrified of the person that not having sex would turn me into; dowdy, frigid, bitter, naive. When I imagined a spinster I saw a woman dead like a spider in the corner, clutching only herself.

So instead of a spinster I became the type of person who ruins parties. I was drunk and reckless, spilled secrets, made scenes. I distributed my phone number like ticker tape at a World Series victory parade. I'd commandeer the sound system and play my favorite sad girl song, "The Rose" by Bette Midler. And of course I'd corner strangers and demand their reactions to, you guessed it, a certain contest of sexual stamina and gluttony. After their initial enthusiasm, I knew my friends were fed up with talk of the 6, 12, 18, 24 challenge. At a party I'd launch into a new line of discussion about pocket rockets or drinking beer from CamelBaks, and out of the corner of my eye catch Elaine slowly lower her head to the bar. Even Margot, whose high school yearbook quote was "Moderation kills the spirit" had reached her limits. I knew they were irritated, but couldn't let it go. Discussing the challenge serviced an existential need that I barely understood. I felt like Maggie Nelson in her memoir *Bluets*, which I obviously read too many times. Like Nelson, my grief-stricken horniness was a "pussy in a serious need of fucking—a pulsing that communicates nothing less than the sucking and ejaculations of the heart."

I could never explain any of this, even to Elaine. There's no story in being unwanted. Instead I'd sink into her Jennifer Convertible and partake in the special comfort of feeling sorry for oneself in the company of a best friend. After I dried my eyes I'd ask about her health and she'd shrug and say, "Oh, you know, big trouble in little vagina."

3:26 p.m.
Filled a Nalgene with three cans of beer. The security guard at the Huntington Gardens didn't suspect a thing.

3:40 p.m.
Tried to order a seven-dollar donut at the cafe, but they
only had the display left and refused to let me buy it. "It's
terrible," the barista told me. "I don't care," I said. He
wouldn't take my money.

4:30 p.m.
Chris and I walked two miles through the bonsai and desert gardens. The gallery was showing the Kihinde Wiley
painting A Portrait of a Young Gentleman. It's done
in the Grand Manner style, a young Black man with
dreads dyed blond at the tip and a tie-dye shirt that grows
into the periwinkle and orange floral backdrop. The man
rests his left hand on his cocked hip and stares across the
hall at Thomas Gainsborough's 1770 portrait, Blue Boy,
which features a white dandy in a blue suit, also posing
with his left hand on his hip. I felt like I was interrupting an argument.

4:50 p.m.
Jerked off in the bathroom at the Japanese garden. I could
hear the bamboo rustling outside and the security guard
telling people that the garden was closing. I did it standing
with my forehead against the clammy brick wall.

Chris and I were the last people at the Huntington,
and we made it to our car just as the sun set. I had been
at the challenge for seven hours and wasn't even halfway
through. The day had slipped away from me.

"What I'm understanding now, is that 12, 18, and 24 are substantial numbers," I texted Cody.

"Yeah, dude!" he replied. "I'm off to bed." It was 9:15 his time and he had to teach early the next morning.

"Thank you for the moral support."

"It's my pleasure."

"Oh, we're way past pleasure."

The records are lost to time, but our best guess is that the 6, 12, 18, 24 challenge began as a bonding exercise for collegiate cross-country teams—the loneliness of the long distance runner and all that. To this day, you can compete in the challenge at Pink Lightning, the runners camp at Burning Man. And this is where the challenge remained—in locker rooms, running subreddits, a desert outside Reno—until 2015, when Dave Portnoy, the face of *Barstool Sports*, live-streamed his attempt.

Portnoy represents everything I hate. He is a frat boy Troy McLure, using his platform to voice support for torture, Trump, the harassment of journalists, vehicular manslaughter, union busting, Tom Brady, a blog post titled "Could Serena Williams Rape You?" He's a forty-four-year-old millionaire pizza blogger who built an empire on the concept that Saturdays aren't for women. Now, there are those who'd contend that I'm not describing Dave Portnoy at all, but rather his alter ego El Presidente. "Not the president of a country but instead a mindset," says Tucker Carlson, another man who insists we respect the distinction between an authoritarian screen persona and, when the broadcast ends, the well-mannered professional simply cashing the checks. As far as I can gather, the Portnoy mindset consists of a day drinker's apathy unless a competition is involved, in which case the necessity of winning can't be overstated. And so when Portnoy announced to his fans that he would attempt the 6, 12, 18, 24 challenge, he meant it.

Portnoy opted for six miles, twelve beers, and a ludicrous eighteen jerk-offs and twenty-four donuts. This is objectively a chump's strategy, but proving the naysayers wrong is what revs Portnoy's engines. "I may even dedicate four jerk-offs to all my doubters and haters," he declared at the start. "That's what gets me excited. That's what gets my dick hard in the morning." He began at night, knocking out six miles and a couple chocolate-glazed donuts. "I'm about to settle in for an extreme jerk-off session," he announced to the thousands of Stoolies following along. #GoPresGo started trending. "I am horrified," tweeted his now ex-wife.

I doubt that Portnoy has an Elaine in his life, someone who sits with him when he's sad, assures him that he's beautiful when no one else will. To me, Portnoy possesses all the sex appeal of a zit with teeth. On some level he must know this; *Barstool Sports* is not the project of a man on joyful terms with the face in the mirror, and truth be told neither is my body of work. I understand what Portnoy was chasing the day he attempted the 6, 12, 18, 24 challenge. It wasn't to show up the doubters and haters, quite the opposite. The challenge has always existed as a form of male bonding, a permission structure that allows men to cheer on each other's ejaculations as they would a favorite sports team. For twenty-four hours, Portnoy could request that his readership care deeply about his penis, that they loyally track its rise and fall, and give his genitals the rarest of alls gifts, unconditional male attention. Don't we all desire an audience?

After the twelve-hour mark, my captain's log becomes morose and ponderous. I had drunk fourteen beers and counting, and my handwriting slid off the margins.

10:20 p.m.
Chris announced I've given him phantom fatigue and has gone to bed. I have to think this would be easier if I wasn't alone. That's the paradox of it. Masturbation is solitary, but crushing beers by yourself is so sad and plodding.

1:35 a.m.
But isn't that the problem of LIFE ITSELF?! We are alone! And yet we need each other! But we are trapped in our individual bodies and moods and impulses and tolerances! And so we desperately seek satisfaction and recognition from others. By which I mean love!

1:54 a.m.
Is this life? Eating and coming and dragging our bodies forward? It's like I think I'm Cool Hand Luke. Remind me, what am I fighting against?

2:40 a.m.
For I have promises to keep, and orgasms to come before I sleep.

In my planning, I had failed to take into account the good-for-nothing daylight savings time shift and the early sunset, and so had only managed to walk three miles. At 3:00 a.m. with seven hours left on the clock, I still needed to have four more beers, eight donuts, eight orgasms, and bang out three miles. The numbers were dire. I was drunk off my ass and hadn't slept at all. For the first time, the challenge felt insurmountable. I slouched on the sofa against a pile of laundry. My only company was a snaggletooth stray cat we were calling Reuben. He had appeared on our doorstep ornery and bloodied and looking like the reincarnation of Bob Hoskins, and had since made himself at home. Every human I knew was asleep.

I considered how I'd feel if I couldn't finish. Perhaps there was nobility in failure. I'd join the ranks of the Jamaican bobsled team, Rocky, the 2001 Yankees. Shackleton was famous not for reaching the South Pole but for watching his ship get crushed by pack ice and surviving anyway. But I just had too many years of big talk and anticipation to live down. Reuben delicately licked his asshole. I cracked my fifteenth beer and rubbed one out under my pajama bottoms.

6:08 a.m.
I closed my eyes for the 17th orgasm and when I opened them, the sun was up.

At 7:00 a.m., I bought four old-fashioneds and four glazed from a place on Sunset that sold donuts and lottery tickets. It was Monday morning, and the only other customers were a construction crew having breakfast. I took my bag of donuts and power walked around Echo Park Lake, eating as I went, lapped by joggers. I wondered if this was my most shameful walk of shame to date. It wasn't how I imagined spending the last days of my twenties. Or maybe it was *exactly* what I imagined doing, just not the way I'd expected to feel. Each bite and every step hit like a self-inflicted punishment, and you'd be forgiven for wondering, as I did that morning, why in the world was I putting myself through this?

After all, the loneliness that drove me into the arms of this challenge had long been solved. I have a loving husband who only a few hours ago had generously shared his special warming lube. Was this my last stand before turning thirty? Or maybe I was trudging around the man-made lake, alone and in pain, because the previous weekend Elaine got married in a ceremony from which I was disinvited, surrounded by a group of friends who I'm no longer on speaking terms with.

It was never about beating the challenge. When I was younger, my loneliness was a humiliation. And so it was a great gift I accepted from my friends, to be allowed to pontificate ad nauseam about vibrators, light beer, clitoral stamina, public indecency. They knew I was working through something. It was an incalculable reassurance that even at my most ragged, Elaine still welcomed me on her Jennifer Convertible. This is one of the greatest mercies a friend can bestow—allowing you to repeat yourself and pretend that they're hearing those thoughts for the first time. Likewise, a friendship is over when your idiosyncrasies and hang-ups, once considered appealing or at worst, a reasonable concession to the worthwhile aspects of your personality, become to your friends—at long last—intolerable.

I hear it, *not another story about a friend breakup*. I'm sorry, but as I've been trying to explain, the 6, 12, 18, 24 challenge is nothing but a feat of repetition. I eat and drink and move and come, the same basic tasks I'll complete over and over for the entirety of my life, some days with others, oftentimes alone. It all takes a toll. Since my early twenties, my hangovers have gotten worse. My fantasies have evolved. (Only the Hitachi has a lifetime warranty.) I moved away, fell in love, got depressed, grieved. Resentments between my friends and I accumulated. Shitty text messages sailed across the country. The fight's details don't matter, and there's no story in being unwanted. It's not my fault that in life you just lose people. (In this particular friend fight, some would say it's precisely my fault, which is of course the point of contention.) I'll admit it, I'm appalled that, from where I stand now, I have a loving partner with a compatible libido and yet all life's problems aren't solved. Likewise, there was a time when I never could have imagined my sex drive would have such definitive limits as the 6, 12, 18, 24 challenge laid bare, or that my knee would be too busted to run on, or that I'd look at a frosty can of beer or hot glazed donut and think, *never again*. Why wouldn't there be limits in friendships as well, including how long they last? Which is why all these years later I found myself in the same position as when I first became obsessed with this thing; bereft and embarrassed—because make no mistake, to lose one's friends is suspect, surely the comeuppance of a reckless person, like someone who leaves their laptop in an unlocked car. My ex–best friends and I used to joke that there's no bigger red flag than someone who begins a sentence with "my ex–best friends." Honestly, if it was possible I'd dig a deep loamy hole in my yard and spend my thirties underground, licking my wounds, recovering from the humiliation. Instead, I tried to walk six miles, eat twelve donuts, drink eighteen beers, and have twenty-four orgasms. It was a game that for some reason I once cared about.

9:27 a.m.
Back at home from the lake. One donut, three Os, 60 minutes to go. Miserable. Alone. Depleted.

Here I stopped writing. The log goes blank.

Later that afternoon I awoke to a dish of baby carrots that Chris left on my bedside table. I showered, and listened to a podcast about William F. Buckley's mayoral run. My brother-in-law wanted to know what to buy for my birthday. I text back: fancy olive oil. Unlike most things we're forced to do, I don't mind growing up. I've found that coming of age is less a matter of *becoming* than of letting go of the more ludicrous notions of who you are. The stinging sensation only comes from breaking the promises made in your youth. Self-negation isn't so bad, though. In fact, we must learn to moderate our impulses, desires, obsessions, lest we turn into Quiz Kid Donnie Smith or El Presidente.

Portnoy conceded his 6, 12, 18, 24 challenge via late-night video. "I lost. Just couldn't jerk off enough," he admitted. He wore a newsboy cap and the kind of plastic sunglasses they hand out at accepted student weekends. "I didn't do this for myself," he continued. "Everything I do is to prove to other people that I'm great. And I failed... I don't care what I think of myself. I know what I think of myself. It's other people." Recently, *Insider* published the accounts of two young women accusing Dave Portnoy of violent and demeaning sexual encounters. One woman who was twenty at the time, said she was screaming in pain and that Portnoy made her feel like "a human sex doll." The other woman, nineteen, said she felt "preyed upon," and three days later was placed under suicide watch. (In response, Portnoy said he had "never done anything that's remotely not consensual." He challenged the credibility of the accusers, and sued *Insider* for invasion of privacy and defamation.) In any event, I don't imagine these women were the "other people" whose opinions Portnoy was concerned about.

For a long time my problem was boys, and I thought the solution would be men. I learned the hard way that loneliness wasn't something I could think my way out of. The 6, 12, 18, 24 challenge on the other hand, could be solved, with cunning and perseverance and skillful masturbation. The challenge gave me a way to talk bawdily about sex in terms that didn't start with my own unfuckability. I fortified my character so as to be unembarrassed by judgment or sexual rejection. When Chris and I met at a bar, he asked what summer movies I was looking forward to and I told him the *Independence Day* sequel, though I'd never seen the original. "Do you want to go watch it right now?" he asked. What a wild line! I laughed in his face! But in his guileless audacity I saw a kindred spirit and within thirty-five minutes the two of us were back at my place and Chris was half-dressed and amicably killing a cockroach on my bedroom wall with his thumb. When exchanging numbers the following morning, I sent him that infamous picture US Airways tweeted out, of a woman fucking herself with a model Boeing 777. "Natalie! No! Why?" moaned Elaine when I told her. Why? I guess because I reached a point where I would either have to change my personality or dig in even deeper. And so I started the work of building a sexual identity measured by dedication and humor and not by the notches on my headboard. In fact, I didn't even have a headboard, just a wall with a window facing west.

We can always take our desires at face value. The 6, 12, 18, 24 challenge is elemental: donuts, beer, distance, jerk-offs. There is nothing more to it than what it is. I spent years overthinking the idea that I had so much love to give and no where to put it. But if you have a surplus of love to give, ain't nothing in the rule book that says you can't self-deal. Sometimes "go fuck yourself" is helpful advice.

So I woke up and decided to walk six miles, eat twelve donuts, drink eighteen beers, and give myself twenty-four orgasms, which you better believe I did, with eight minutes to spare. This is not a story about loneliness! This is not entirely a story about loneliness! Sticktoitiveness is a form of courage, and actually, the promises you made in your youth deserve to be honored. Don't let anyone convince you otherwise. When the night has been too lonely and the road has been too long, and you think that love is only for the lucky and the strong, you can always take matters into your own hands.

ADULT DRAMA
OR
THE VIRGIN CUNT CLUB

"This is all *I ever wanted," I lied.* That would have been the first line of Caroline Calloway's memoir. At least the draft I was writing in 2017, before our collaboration ended, as they often do, in competing narratives. My version of her life story opened on teenage Caroline in her boyfriend's bed at boarding school. She has just had sex for the first time and is wondering if the life she always wanted for herself is actually the life she wants. She doesn't know yet that in order to change she'll have to take her "sweet, stupid past self" behind the barn and shoot her. All she knows for sure is that when she tells the story of her life (and she *will* tell the story of her life), she'll begin right here, when she felt the "urgent, clear directive: go." Without waking her boyfriend to say good-bye, she climbs out of the window of the dorm and drops to the winter ground with a soft crunch. The sun is rising. She's the only one on campus awake. And she sets off, *"the snowy field stretching before me like the pages of an unwritten story."*

It's a joke now, the idea that anything about Caroline has gone unwritten. Since we met, almost a decade ago, the revisions and retellings have kept piling up. We became friends in creative nonfiction class, cowrote Instagram captions introducing Caroline (or a character named Caroline) to an online audience, and because Caroline is a writer who often, in lieu of writing, creates her character by living, when we sold a book proposal based off those captions we never came close to finishing the book, and so I wrote my own personal essay about it all, for which I received an obscene and life-changing amount of attention that I leveraged into money to buy myself more time to write, this time about myself. Since then there have been documentaries, think pieces, *discourse*, a robust subreddit. A publicly traded company owns my life rights, and a very talented showrunner has been hard at work turning my essay about Caroline into a limited series, because at this point, what's the harm in one or two more adaptations?

I had always told myself I didn't want to be an art monster. If I ever did write about Caroline, it would be under a pen name, and I'd change her name, too, and I'd publish it somewhere so obscure that no one would run the risk of ever reading it. It's also true that I keep a copy of *The Journalist and the Murderer* in my bedside table next to my ChapStick. The writer's subject must "face the fact that the journalist—who seemed so friendly and sympathetic, so keen to understand him fully, so remarkably attuned to his vision of things—never had the slightest intention of collaborating with him on his story," writes Janet Malcolm, "but always intended to write a story of his own." I can only feign innocence.

When we worked together, Caroline often made the argument that she was entitled to write about whomever she wanted—friends, classmates, boyfriends both former and current. When I visited her in Cambridge, a group of future world leaders who had spent a night doing drugs with Caroline threatened legal action if she went ahead with her plan to publish a photo of all of them partying. In awe, I watched as Caroline stood her ground.

I, too, was surreptitiously taking notes, and what writer takes notes without a plan to use them? Like Caroline, I'm an unreliable narrator. I'll adjust the truth at the margins in service of a sentence. I hoard the stories of those closest to me like a contestant on *RuPaul's Drag Race* grabbing shower curtains during an unconventional materials design challenge. I didn't come here to make friends.

Which is all to say, in retrospect my betrayal of Caroline seems inevitable. What then does that say about the years we counted each other as real friends? Was it all bullshit? Pragmatically, you could argue that I used Caroline as a subject just as she used me as an editor and ghostwriter. Maybe we were compatriots for a time, but not friends so much as collaborators in the projects of our separate lives. That's why when I eventually decided to write and publish that essay on Caroline, her real name included, it was easy to think of her as just my subject, or otherwise a former boss who owed me back wages.

Lately, I have grown terrified that I no longer know the difference between a person meaningfully growing and changing, or just rebranding themselves. I am worried I confuse brand loyalty for friendship. And that the most genuine relationship most of us have is with our phone, where everything we say and look at makes someone else money. You feel it, too, right? In an attention marketplace that has made a memoirist out of almost all of us, and if all memoirists are duplicitous, can we trust any relationship? But there I go again, hiding behind the first-person plural. What I mean is, can I trust myself?

Back when I sold the television rights to the essay, the executives I met were all effusive and prepared—I had something they wanted—as they pitched me their version of my story. *Single White Female* meets *Eighth Grade*. Gender-swapped *Talented Mr. Ripley*. *The Bold Type* but they want to kill each other. More than one VP asked me, pen poised over legal pad: "What *genre* do you see yourself in?"

I still don't know the answer to that question, despite

the fact that as we speak, the showrunner is working away on a television show featuring a character with my name and backstory. Even money it'll be a snappy bildungsroman. Creatively, a coming-of-age dramedy makes sense—form reflects content—even if I'm exhausted by the genre. How many times am I expected to come of age? For once, grant me an adult drama. Let my character wear a tailored suit and hold in her tears. Give me a story where each day isn't a hormonal catastrophe, where every personality isn't an open wound. What if I didn't need to go on another journey of self-discovery because I already knew who I was? And if I'm not running around constantly wondering *Who am I?*, what else might I think about?

As a condition of the TV deal, I'm obligated to provide the production with supporting material—early essay drafts and emails, even my diaries I suppose, which I feel I'd have to hand over in a lead box the way plutonium is transported. I've sat for a few interviews in the showrunner's sunroom. She starts a recording app on her phone and asks me what kind of shoes I wore back then, my politics, my body image, the books I read, the vibes of my childhood home. (This is an extremely flattering process, throughout which I disregard everything Janet Malcolm warned me about.) Most of all, the showrunner and I talk about my decision to finally turn the tables and write about myself instead of as Caroline— my workspace, my process, when and why did I decide to write it, how did I choose where to start the story? To fully answer her questions I have to dig into the archive, which paralyzes me with dread. What do I think will happen when I look back at emails from 2015? I'll turn to salt?

The only part of my book draft that Caroline said she'd keep were the sections I wrote about the two of us. As in life, in the book we meet on the first day of a creative nonfiction class. Caroline sees me, or the character based off me, as unthreatening, with her freckles and "meek little ponytail" (a description I'd reuse in my own essay). The twist is that I'm the workshop bitch. When Caroline presents her piece to the class, an essay about her first boyfriend that she's confident is a masterpiece, I give myself the villain edit. I judge her essay as childish and grandiose, and ask why she opted for run-on sentences and alliteration in lieu of self-awareness. "You write about your prep school boyfriend the way Walt Whitman writes about Lincoln," I tell her.

In real life, I wasn't so harsh, but when crafting the scene, I knew Caroline needed a caustic foil. Maybe there was part of me that saw an opportunity to Trojan-Horse my criticism of Caroline into her own book. Maybe I was subconsciously confessing. In any event, it was important to the story that I was an asshole, if only to make what happens next matter.

My workshop critique obliterates Caroline's confidence. In this telling, I am so formidable and Caroline, in comparison, fragile as a baby bird, that I send her into an existential tailspin. "You're not actually a writer," she thinks to herself. (A complete fabrication on my part. I'm not a mind reader.) Her internal monologue goes on: "No one cares about the first time you had sex and how small you felt afterwards… That stuff was dumb when it happened and it was dumb when it was retold." I've broken her. Caroline refuses to even read the notes I wrote on her draft. In fact, she abandons her dreams of becoming a writer all together, and gives up on the fantasy of life in New York.

But wait, there's a second twist, which is that actually all I ever wanted was to help Caroline become the best writer she could be! In the chapter's climatic scene, Caroline visits my Gowanus apartment and sees firsthand my precarious stacks of paperbacks and the hole hammered through the drywall. I explain that I read *Just Kids* and thought if I wanted to be a real New York artist, then I need exposed brick. We talk, and Caroline admits that she thought her boyfriend essay was perfect, but after the rough workshop she had given it up. I respond, "Oh god that depresses me. The idea of being twenty and writing something you feel you can't make better." When she confesses she didn't read my notes, I tell her that good notes are a gift, and she shouldn't take an editor for granted. Later that night Caroline digs out the draft with my line edits and annotations. She assumed it would be horribly mean, a list of reasons why she should never write again. But after reading them, Caroline learns that "good notes are the opposite. They urge you forward." We end on Caroline's realization, "when you find a good editor, never let her go. Same with a good friend. Natalie became both."

In the essay I published in *The Cut*, I don't make it explicit why I decided to finally write about Caroline. Reading the piece, you might have come away with the impression that one day I felt melancholy and introspective and put pen to paper. Or maybe I had been reading about Caroline in the news, and like an old woman who writes the newspaper identifying minor grammatical errors, I felt duty bound to correct the public record. Or maybe I wasn't as adept at hiding my true feelings as I thought I was. The truth wasn't so bloodless.

In short, fury consumed me. In the two years since we had stopped speaking, I had tried to put Caroline out of my head, but when she resurfaced at the top of 2019 with those creativity workshops, I felt my unexpressed feelings turn gangrenous. All those years I had spent serving Caroline's artistic vision. Obsequious as a Claude Raines character. I turned myself into any literary device she needed while barely writing anything of my own. Why was Caroline never anxious that I'd write about her? Did she forget that I was a memoirist, too? Did she think that I didn't have the killer instinct? Maybe she failed to see the distinction between the real me and the character I wrote for myself in her book. The Natalie on the page would never sell Caroline out. That version of me defines herself not as a writer but editor, and exists solely to provide literary support and the occasional pithy remark. In real life, my POV threatened to burn a hole through my forehead like a third eye.

I remember a moment when I was visiting Cambridge: Caroline sat at her vanity, surrounded by French perfumes and serums, and while gazing at her face asked me, "Do you ever think to yourself, 'I might be the most beautiful girl in the world'?" When I decided to write the essay, I felt like Caroline must have at that mirror. Only, when I looked at my reflection I thought, "I could write the hell out of this story. I could take it from her. It could be mine."

If Caroline had ever taken the 1 train up to Gaelic Park to see me play college soccer, she might have understood who she was dealing with. Or maybe I was the one who needed reminding. I could forget who I became on the field, like how they say you don't remember the intensity of childbirth. It's a feeling of grit and turf burn, wiping blood from my knee with the back of my hand. As a captain, sometimes it was my job to pick out a player on the opposing team, the girl causing us problems, and knock her flat on the Astroturf so she knew. Talking about those bygone days can make me feel trapped in a mournful Springsteen song, although that sense of competition isn't just a fond memory but a reflex my body retains. It's a glint in the eye. A refusal to get beaten by some bitch from Carnegie Mellon.

This sensation of gathering power is elusive—especially for those of us who spend most of our time hunched over our desks—and it's important to pay attention to, lest you wind up like that guy who ruptured his throat holding in a sneeze. It was an overcast January morning and I was at the 101 Coffee Shop with friends, overcaffeinated and enraged. I smacked my hand down on the Formica table. "Fuck it!" I screeched. "I'm writing about her."

When I originally pitched, it was supposed to be a different kind of story. It was a couple weeks later and I was standing outside the Salt Lake City Airport, my back turned against the wind. "I was her ghostwriter! Sort of! For, like years!" I shouted into my phone to editors at *The Cut*. My cold cheek kept pressing random keys on my phone, and for stretches of the call all I heard on the other end were discordant beeps. I was in town for Sundance having played a small role in convincing my bosses to represent the Alexandria Ocasio-Cortez documentary *Knock Down the House*, and I'd spend the next ten days making powerful film executives undrinkable cups of coffee. My original essay pitch was a political tirade against white girl hypocrisy. This was the top of 2019, you remember the news cycle: Brett Kavanaugh had just been confirmed, the UN forecasted climate apocalypse, birthright citizenship was up for debate, police kept murdering Black people, incels kept murdering women, and in the midst of all this Caroline was now publicly a lefty feminist. I could have been happy for her political growth, or recognized her leftward shift as identical to my own. Instead, I interpreted it as nothing more than an opportunistic rebrand.

When we worked together, Caroline insisted that her account was apolitical. I disagreed. Whether Caroline cared to admit it, I argued that #Adventuregrams was inherently transgressive. *Don't you get it, Caroline?* I'd shout. *Female confessional writing is radical, it's consciousness raising, for godsakes it's praxis!* I deeply believed this at the time. That writing honest first-person narration was *doing the work.* And so later when all our white girl memoirs had failed to slow the collapse of democracy, the story I wanted to put in *The Cut* wasn't about how I ghostwrote Caroline's *memoir,* but her self-serving politics. In a follow-up email to the deputy editor, I wrote, "Self-delusion needs enablers, and I was literally crafting a false public persona with her. I ate lunch with Donald Trump's agent, worked with him, told Caroline she was a feminist simply by telling her own story… Caroline [and I] and so many white women need to hold ourselves accountable."

My editor gently suggested I tone down my Sorkin moment and keep the story personal; emotions and relationships, a girl finding her voice. I think this pivot made the essay better. Undoubtedly, more commercial. But I wonder if I gave up my political critique too easily. I had a valid point, right? About how privileged girls co-opt liberation politics to build our brands? On one hand, I wouldn't have been breaking any news with this take. On the other, I gave up my political critique of self-mythologizing white girls to instead become another self-mythologizing white girl.

No one should go viral. Our egos are too greedy, our brains too fragile. It is an excruciating waste of time and nerves, and my only advice on the matter would be, if at all possible, trade your moment in the spotlight for something in return, preferably the means to be unbothered and offline in the near future.

When my essay about Caroline landed, we became the main characters of the internet. My inbox swelled with media requests, hate mail, sob stories, well-wishes, considered critique, vitriol. There was drama in the pencil community, an editorial oversight involving lettuce wraps. I wondered why so many adults were obsessing over a story about a friendship breakup between two girls, and I had to remind myself that I was also an adult, and had cared enough to write it. The *New Haven Register* published a "local girl goes viral" story. A columnist for *The Atlantic* called me a "poison diarist" writing a "revenge essay." A photo of my sister circulated as me. Reporters called my old employers and for some reason I told the paper of record about losing my virginity. When I wrote the essay, I wanted to preserve the story's nuance, but Caroline and I were instantaneously flattened into a blonde vs. brunette binary—"Are you a Caroline or a Natalie?" asked a *BuzzFeed* quiz. Taking it, I was relieved to learn I was still myself, but even that was becoming a fuzzier concept.

I had become, it appeared, a brand. Scam victim, social media survivor, casualty of pretty privilege, spokesman for nebbishy friends everywhere. People seemed to want that story from me, not just teens asking advice but producers making documentaries about online fame, YA publishers soliciting novelizations of my story. A magazine editor offered good money to commission my take on Olivia Jade. A booker for Dr. Phil tried valiantly to get me on the show to talk about "influencers and their relationships with family/friends and loved ones." I called out of work and spent the next day lying facedown on the couch, vibrating with anxiety. I was reminded of the locust swarms described in Caroline Fraser's biography of Laura Ingalls Wilder, "a mystifying cloud had darkened the clear sky of southwest Minnesota...it was flickering red, with silver edges, and appeared to be alive, arriving at 'racehorse speed.'" Once they made landfall, the locusts settled a foot thick over the farms, devouring not just the crops but the sweat-stained handles of farm tools and the wool off sheep—"everything but the mortgage"—the sound of their chewing like "thousands of scissors cutting and snipping." Surely I was overreacting, but even when I logged off, I swear I could still feel the cloud of scrutiny just outside my field of vision.

I really did try to be fair to Caroline. My initial anger was useful in jolting me out of writer's block (a euphemism for depression), but once I started the draft, I had to face the fact that I was far from the innocent victim of a hot girl. My diary entries and old emails told a different story, where I was manipulative and slippery. Like Caroline, I played a shell game with my affections. I never wasn't taking notes. Time and time again I diminished myself as a strategy to get what I wanted, which worked because for many years Caroline and I wanted the same thing. Then we didn't. This is all to say, when I finally dug into the writing, I wanted to be generous and understanding to Caroline on the page, for the sake of the work and her well-being, which of course I cared about, despite that I knew writing about her would unleash a level of attention that can crush a person flat. I truly believed that as long as I wrote the both of us as complicated and messy, tempered my pluck with self-loathing, and remained true to my memory and the archive, that in the end we would come out unscathed.

My first ever friend was a girl I'll call Julie. There are pictures of us swaddled as newborns lying side by side. Childhood was essentially one long playdate and there wasn't a time when we weren't best friends. Sisters actually, fraternal twins, teammates, confidantes, close as two people can be. Things changed in high school, slowly at first. I began to understand that while life for me came easily enough—friendships and soccer, optimism, as much self-assuredness as a teenage girl could reasonably hope for, Julie had a harder time. I didn't understand yet that happiness could be harder for some people to keep hold of. In ninth grade, I wrote a little comedic essay: two fifteen-year-old girls talk in the cafeteria. One is having a meltdown about the Bush administration, child soldiers, the inescapable evil of the world. The other, nonplussed, takes in her friend's tirade while eating an escalating assortment of lunch meats. The essay won me attention of the lit mag, assembly reading sort; older classmates read it and thought I was funny and cool, a compliment that from then on I'd never stop chasing. Truthfully, the two characters in the essay were separate halves of myself, but I thought Julie would be flattered to be written into my success, so I told her that the second girl, the unbothered one, was based on her. Turns out, Julie did not consider her portrayal as my dull sounding board to be an honor, and the food jokes touched a nerve. I knew I'd hurt her feelings. Anyway, years passed. We went to college on separate coasts and stayed close even as we grew apart. On school breaks, often when we were drunk and teary, I caught glimpses of trouble, but was still shocked when the summer after our sophomore year Julie ended up in the ICU.

I blamed myself for everything—a lifetime of fucking up with my own selfishness, epitomized by that stupid essay. What's the point of friendship if not to keep each other alive? By Julie's bedside, I promised myself that from then on I would be so perfect a friend I would shield her from despair.

Coincidentally, when Julie was in the hospital, Caroline was in New Haven for a Yale writing program. At that point we had only known each other for a semester, and when I picked her up from Union Station it felt incongruous to see her in my hometown, like running into a fictional character at the supermarket. It was weirder still when I dropped her off at her dorm, and she introduced me to the RA as her older sister. Anyway, a couple days later I met Caroline outside the hospital so I could take a break from sitting with Julie.

"Just to let you know, I have a sore throat so I can't talk much," Caroline announced as we cut through downtown. "How are you?"

I told her about how rough it was in the hospital. The

guilt I felt over all of it. That I'd spent the last few nights getting drunk off my parents' Blue Moon and replaying every mistake I'd ever made in our friendship. I felt like crying all the time, but I also felt like it was my job to be the friend that didn't cry, the one who could hold everything together.

Caroline walked beside me and listened to every word. After a beat she said, "I don't actually have a sore throat. I was just pretending to get you to open up."

A few months later I started writing for her.

In the final draft of *The Cut* essay I kept out some details, mostly gossip and menstrual secrets.

For example, when I prepared Caroline's apartment for her first Airbnb guest, I didn't just find trash on the floor, but dried period blood all over her bedding. (Caroline has since publicly written about this, which I'm telling myself is the only reason I'm writing about it now.) I had been sexually assaulted the night before, and instead of spiriting away the soiled bedding to the laundry or trash chute, I angrily stuffed the blanket between the bed and the wall, let the guest in, and left for the day. Over the next several hours I received and ignored frantic messages from Caroline and then her mother, begging me to go fix the menstrual blood situation that the guest was not happy about.

Truthfully, I could barely believe it myself when I saw the bloody scene Caroline had left me. I mean, the gall, but what an image. Even after the night I had just lived through, the writer in me saw the mess and thought when it comes to a metaphor, one simply cannot beat period blood on a white comforter—pain, guts, renewal, the feminine grotesque, baby! Years before we met, my husband, Chris, was hooking up with a girl at a roof-top party when she reached under her skirt, pulled out her tampon, and flung it off the side of the building. Just imagine, the swollen tampon arcing through the night sky. Landing wetly on the sidewalk. Inner work-ings made visible. In my work, I try to be exact in my sentence construction, to design graceful Aristotelian arcs and build upon each draft like a bridge across an expanse of water, but it strikes me that bleeding out is just as valid a way to tell a story.

When Julie was discharged from the hospital, my com-mitment to care for her often took the form of lying to protect her feelings. More likely, I was lying to keep my-self from becoming the judgmental friend, her enemy.

When Julie caught me in one such lie and our friend-ship ended, I was hemorrhaging blood. At the time I was twenty-one and had only been getting my period a couple times a year, a symptom of infertility or cervical cancer I assumed, proof that on the inside I was rotten. The university health center gave me a progesterone tab-let and told me they'd only worry if I went two weeks without menstruating, and wouldn't you know it, on Christmas morning I woke up in my childhood bed soaked through with blood. It was like I was sleeping on a fresh crime scene. Later that day Julie and I fought be-cause I had lied about a party I secretly didn't invite her to. She ended things over text, telling me she no longer wanted to be a member of my "Virgin Cunt Club"— a line better than anything I could ever hope to write.

Lately, I've been having this waking nightmare where I'm a contestant ambushed on *Billy on the Street*. Billy chases after me screaming, "MISS, FOR A DOLLAR NAME A THING THAT HAS HAPPENED TO YOU" and I'm only able to sputter, "Caroline Calloway!"

It seems harder these days to write a personal essay that's not a thesis of self, with all the narrative logic of the "Our Story" section on a corporate website. Everything feels like a soft launch of a podcast or for that matter, IP for a TV series. (I guess you could resist the self-promotional impulse by publishing your most disgusting secrets, but come on, that's what pimple-popping videos are there for.) I was reading Jenny Odell's book *How to Do Nothing: Resisting the Attention Economy* in fall 2019, the exact moment I became a hot commodity in the attention economy. To turn yourself into a brand, Odell writes, is to preclude yourself from the possibility of "change, ambiguity, and contradiction" at the expense of "the carnal and the poetic." This is good for business interests, as a predictable entity can be easily converted into a unit of capital ("Are you a Caroline or a Natalie?"), but it's socially cataclysmic. "If we recognize that what we experience as the self is completely bound to others, determined not by essential qualities but by relationships, then we must further relinquish the idea of a controllable identity and of a neutral, apolitical existence," Odell argues. Writer Ayesha Siddiqi says, "How you treat people is who you are... Your choices leave a record." A record I think, that's kept on the bodies of other people.

As a writer, I don't know what to do with this. I agree with Joy Williams when she says, "There is something unwholesome and destructive about the entire writing process." This is from her essay "Uncanny Singing that Comes from Certain Husks." She goes on, "A writer starts out, I think, wanting to be a transfiguring agent, and ends up usually just making contact, contact with other human beings. This, unsurprisingly, is not enough."

What I wrote about Caroline was both destructive and not enough. Particularly the moment in my essay when Caroline tells me if I write the book without her, she'll commit suicide. When I was working on the draft, I couldn't figure out how to explain the end of our relationship without that exchange. Everything changed for me, after suicide entered the conversation. I remember standing barefoot in my kitchen after the call ended, feeling helpless, and then feeling liberated by my helplessness. I thought, how am I supposed to work under these conditions? The answer was I couldn't. In fact, Caroline just explicitly forbid me from doing the work. She had set me free. Two years later, I published a paraphrased account of the conversation. I brushed aside misgivings. Being delicate had gotten me nowhere. I told myself that getting the story right would be a moral victory in and of itself.

A few days after the essay went up, I was still on the couch, recording a podcast interview when the news came out that Caroline's father had killed himself. I said something like "I can't do this" and hung up. I felt responsible. When I decided to write the essay, I reasoned that I wasn't dragging Caroline into a public sphere she didn't willingly inhabit already. I didn't consider the collateral damage. I put a spotlight on her family. I had fired a gun in the air and the bullet had come down.

Later I learned that he had died before the piece came out, but I still couldn't shake the lingering sense of culpability. Other people's lives aren't content—only, if you do what I do, of course they are.

In her response, Caroline wrote, "Of all the stinging insults and intimate secrets Natalie published about me one hurts more than anything else: She made my suicidal ideation part of the public record." She goes on to say, "I talk about suicide openly now that everyone knows, and it turns out it's not even as bad as I thought it would be. But I wish I had been able to make the choice of when to share that part of me with the world. And I really wish Natalie hadn't made it the punchline of a joke."

As I've worked on this second essay about Caroline, I've wondered if I'm just trying to manufacture a last laugh. Only there's no such thing, just as there's no good way to end a memoir, short of elegantly dropping dead after you write the final sentence. Way back when Caroline and I made our first attempt at the book proposal, when we were in our early twenties and stayed awake for two straight days and ate nothing but Adderall, I wrote as Caroline:

> The story of your life does not end. It's a problem for memoirists, and especially those of us telling these stories online. I assumed that when stories end they stay that way. But then, the story I'm telling of my life just keeps going and going, and just when I think I've reached the end—of a chapter, a boy, a particular sense of longing—the story shakes itself off and follows me out the door. So, how do you end something? I guess you have to kill it.

This was the point of the night, it should be noted, that I was hallucinating garden tools. I hardly remember writing this, and it certainly wasn't included in the pitch we'd sell a few months later. In fact, I wasn't even writing the proposal anymore. Instead, I was trying to solve the problem, as I perceived it, of Caroline's character. I was trying to resolve a narrative arc for the real person sitting across from me. (And all these years I thought I was the one who got flattened on the page.) In my own voice, I wrote:

> How specifically can Caroline the character change in response to the journey she has been on? She can take a deep read of the story she's been telling about herself for the past few years. She can sift through the record, look for clues, moments of clarity and revelation, where she can see the control exerted

over the narrative by the authorial voice—which interesting enough is her own voice, obscuring the truth, playing the role of the antagonist to her future self's protagonist.

To be sure, these are the ramblings of a stoned person who suspects she has spontaneously become a genius. I think what I was reaching for: a careful rereading of the story we tell about ourselves is a good way to change for the better. The villain in your life now is made from the lies you once told about yourself.

In the unfinished book, authority figures keep asking Caroline to "explain yourself." For cutting class to party throughout Europe, for lying on LinkedIn about her internships at Gagosian and Christie's. It was a framing device, the idea being that the book itself was Caroline's explanation of why she was the way she was. As her collaborator, I thought if I tried hard enough, I could figure out who Caroline was, and when I did that, I could write her memoir and I don't know, save her life. The problem was, she never asked me to save her life. For that matter, she never asked me to write her memoir. I just knew that if I didn't no one would, and it would have all been for nothing.

I spent so many years wondering—at times, obsessing over—why she behaved the way she did, where would she wind up. It was this curiosity back when we met that started this whole thing. Who is this girl? Let me stick

around and find out. As if it's possible to truly know anyone, let alone Caroline Calloway.

She told me she had wanted to be an actor, and only
abandoned the idea when she realized she'd have to work
her way up through bit parts, like the one she said she had
in the 2007 Nicole Kidman movie *The Invasion*. I actually saw *The Invasion* by accident, when the theater usher
bounced my underage friends and me from *Superbad*. I
remember it as a lifeless remake of *Invasion of the Body
Snatchers*, itself a paranoid classic about lifeless remakes.
(And perhaps ghostwriting.) Caroline told me she played
a girl who hands a piece of space debris to a government
official, but she was cagey and changed subjects whenever I asked for details. She's listed in the credits under a
different name, she told me, it was no big deal, she didn't
remember much of the shoot. Over the years I'd assumed
this was another one of her incomprehensible but harm-
less lies. But recently I rewatched *The Invasion* and there
Caroline was, four minutes in. At least I think that's her.
We only see her from behind. She's young, and is wearing a flannel shirt with her hair half up. In the scene, she
approaches a CDC bigwig as he exits the testing facility
where he just learned that the space debris that crashed
to earth is covered in alien spores. Caroline—the girl I
think is Caroline—stops him in his town car and hands
him a piece of metal. "Sir? This was on our roof," she
says. The CDC director reaches for it and cuts his finger and that night fungus encases his face and he spends
the rest of the movie using the full might of the CDC

to spread the infection via flu vaccines (yikes!), turning people so sane that they're crazy. After that, Caroline disappears from the movie. I couldn't tell you what I was searching for, but I watched the scene over and over.

As I've told it, when it came time to write the book, Caroline wrote nothing. This is mostly true. Certainly true from the perspective of the agents and editors and publishers. What to make, then, of the forty thousand words about her senior year of high school that she wrote over several sleepless days without stopping, Jack Kerouac style? Of everything I have saved from that time, this is the one that haunts me. Because the draft, or whatever you want to call it, is brilliant! Utterly unsalvageable, self-indulgent, manic, at times unintelligible, but all the same, it rips. When I first read it, I was jealous. Then I was furious, because it only confirmed what I'd always believed: together we could have written a solid book. And by herself, Caroline can write a great book, maybe the book she always imagined. "Every time you told a story was a chance to feel close to someone," she wrote about being the new girl at boarding school. As I do in my draft notes, here Caroline often slips into the second person. It's as if her high school self was in the room with her, hearing the story of how she came to be. Like when Caroline writes that seeing a good photo of herself would "brighten you inside like a compliment," not out of vanity, but because the photo served as "evidence that the world was seeing you the way you wanted to be seen."

When Caroline sent this to me we were in the last,

frantic weeks of trying to pull together a book draft. So
I combed through the document, which again, was sen-
sational and harrowing and unusable, and I pulled out all
the lines I thought could work in the book, lines like,
"You have homework due and he has homework due, but
there is always homework due the same way there is always
weather." This was a fool's errand. The fact of the matter
was, the book I was writing for Caroline was meant to be
slick and palatable, the kind of thing you'd leaf through in
the checkout line at Urban Outfitters. By contrast this document read like Caroline was performing her own open-
heart surgery. I know how bullish that sounds. The pages
were still a mess, but in all the time I'd known Caroline,
I had never seen her as clearly as through this writing. For
once, she had written past her layers of self-protection, and
transported us to her time in high school, those desperate
and banal moments between class, the constant yearning,
the half-drunk Diet Coke bottles in her dorm room and
the "plunking sound they made as you threw them in the
empty trashcan," and how when you're growing up "all you
want is to be okay and hear the world at a normal volume."

I'll stop. No writer wants their early drafts shared, especially by embittered former collaborators. Just returning to the document feels like a trespass. When I reread
it, I can finally understand why Caroline tanked her book
deal rather than allow me to finish the manuscript. Like
me, she never aspired to be a brand. She wanted to write
a memoir that was so perfect it would have reconstructed
the emotional landscapes of her past. She wanted the
kind of girls who read book acknowledgements to pick

up her memoir and feel exactly what she felt when she was younger, and by doing so know they aren't alone. She wanted evidence that world saw her as she saw herself, which as long as I knew her, was a writer.

Back to the problem then, of how to end a memoir. How about with a short little story I've never figured out how to tell. I had just graduated high school and a few good friends and I spent a summer weekend in a cabin up north. With a kitchen to ourselves, we cooked marijuana into butter and made brownies, only to misjudge the servings and become a group of deeply stoned and paranoid city kids convinced the forest was out to devour us. The cabin had no running water and late at night I was forced outside to pee. I walked deep into the trees. I felt more alone than I ever had. I squatted, pulled the string of my tampon, and not knowing what to do with it, flung it into the brush. The next morning I awoke in bed with a clear mind. I realized that the previous night I only walked ten feet from the cabin, and now my bloody tampon was sitting out there for all my friends to see. I ran outside to hide the evidence and found it right away, the tampon nestled in the grass and covered in *slugs*. What's more, the slugs had sucked the tampon clean, and now it was white and bright as fresh cotton.

Every true story is disgusting.

The relationship between Caroline and myself is impossible to explain, but that's the case with most relationships. When our friendship ended it left an absence. I know it was real because it still hurts.

So anyway, I flung the tampon covered in slugs into the woods and thought to myself, *no one will ever know. I will take this hideous secret to my grave.* But just a couple hours later on the drive back to New Haven, hands on the wheel, I couldn't help myself. I announced to my friends in the car, "You won't believe what just happened…" Whatever that story meant, it was mine to tell.

★ ★ ★ ★ ★

ACKNOWLEDGMENTS

I live and work on the traditional, ancestral, and unceded territory of the Gabrielino-Tongva peoples.

I had the great privilege of collaborating with two generous and exacting editors. John Glynn at Hanover Square Press took a chance on this book at a time when no one else did. He guided me through self-doubt, missed deadlines, and cringey first drafts. Every first-time author should be so lucky. And to the iconic Carrie Frye, I'd be lost without you.

I wouldn't be in a position to write this book if it weren't for the extraordinary team at *New York Magazine*. I'd especially like to thank Ruth Spencer, Genevieve Smith, Stella Bugbee, Jane Drinkard, Ted Hart,

Preeti Kinha, Liane Radel, Katy Schneider, and Madison Malone Kircher.

I am grateful for the opportunity to try out early drafts for the blog *Indoor Voices*. Special thanks to Kyle Chayka for the title "Dead People's Stuff."

Thank you to everyone at Hanover Square Press. Thank you to the HarperCollins Union for taking a stand. Thank you to the librarians at the Los Angeles Public Library and the good people at Stories Books and Cafe and Skylight Books.

Thank you to Gabrielle Lewis, Berni Barta, Mollie Glick, Cait Hoyt, Jiah Shin, and Justine Shah. Thank you to Bethany Haynes, Amy Bickersteth, Shari Hosaki, Brendan Healey, and Dominique Previlon. Attention must be paid to the support staff who are worked harder than the rest of us, including but not limited to Eden Railsback, Eris Doble, Michael Zalta, Julien Smith, Alexa Rozansky, Lola Bellier, Michael Johnston, Via Romano, Lili Cohen, and Adi Mehr.

Thank you to Mary South, Amanda Montell, and Rachel Yoder for the support and inspiration. Thank you to Leigh Haber for your mentorship. I am humbled by the opportunity to work alongside Halley Feiffer, Scott Robertson, and Ryan Murphy.

I am indebted to my brilliant and loving friends, who make life worth it and whose fingerprints are all over these pages: Ben, Cleo, Evan, Gaby, Graham, Jennalee, Jocelyn, Kerry, Kiran, Lisa, Liv, Matt, Maya, Michelle, Sydney, Taylor, Tina, Will, and all the rest of you. I love you.

Thank you to Rosanna Kvernmo for your thoughtful notes and for hiring me when I needed a port in the storm. Thank you to Blake Butler for your generosity.

I would be nothing without the teachers who have come through my life. I'm especially grateful for learning from Barbara Sasso, Rachel Sexton, Caroline Rosenstone, Arnie Sabatelli, Nastaran Ahmadi, Michelle Canning, Rinne Groff, and Sophie Lewis. Shout out to New Haven public school and the Educational Center for the Arts.

Thank you to my team: Dusty, Reuben, Marge, and Clarence, a nice dog. Thank you to Aaron Judge for 2022.

I can't express my gratitude to my family. To my aunt Lucy, thank you for taking me under your wing. To my parents, Jennifer and Randy—you've always been my writing role models. I'd be nothing without you guys, which is obvious, but I still should say it more often. Thank you to my brilliant sister, Charlotte, the epitome of a ride or die. I can't wait to see where the road takes us. And to my husband, Chris, you rock my world. Thank you for *everything*.